500 MORE FUCHSIAS

500 More Fuchsias

Miep Nijhuis

B.T. Batsford Ltd . London

First published in Great Britain 1996

ISBN 0 7134 7941 8

Originally published under the title *Vijfhonderd Fuchsia's te kijk* © 1995 by Uitgeverij J.H. Gottmer/H.J.W. Becht BV, Postbus 160, 2060 AD Bloemendaal, The Netherlands

Printed in Holland

Photography by:
B. Aalhuizen, F. van der Elshout, Kwekerij Franken, J. Kamphuis, J. de Nie, C. Spek, A. van Wijk

Cover photographs:
Julicka, Orangeblossom, Fairy Tales, Len Bielby, Delta's Paljas, *F. juntasensis,* Big Slim, Truus Gottmer, Buga '91, Martin's Yellow Surprise, Zet's Alpha, Jaspers Groentje, Mini, Obergartner Koch, Hilda, Walz Lucifer, Herzilein

Foreword

After the enormous success of 1000 Fuchsias there was great demand for more! In fact, 500 Fuchsias can be seen not only as a continuation of the earlier compilation but also - indeed primarily - as a selection standing in its own right. There is no overlap between the two books - both contain a range of well known and less well known cultivars, and will appeal alike to the novice and the experienced fuchsia enthusiast.

Some of the plants in the book will be new to many readers - not least because many growers concentrate on 'easy' plants, and these tend to be the most easily available. We hope that the range of fuchsias shown here will be a revelation. We have included many of the latest new cultivars from Holland and Belgium. Britain, Germany and France, too, are increasingly active in producing new varieties, which will excite and amaze the fuchsia-lover.

The plants in the photographs are arranged in order of colour. After the photographic section, all the plants are described in detail, arranged in alphabetical order by name, and cross-referenced to the pictures. After that there are detailed lists: all the fuchsias described and illustrated are not only listed for easy reference under their different colour headings, but also according to other properties. For example, you may be looking for a white/purple trailer, easy to grow: in the list headed 'white/purple' you find all the suitable candidates from the colour point of view; then, under 'suitable for baskets' you will find all the hanging varieties together; finally you look under 'easy to grow' to see whether one of your white/purple favourites figures there.

Fuchsia growers today are tending to choose and arrange on the basis of colour, especially for tubs and basket: these lists will be an invaluable aid to plant- and garden-lovers. Similarly, lovers of big, double flowers or those who prefer smaller, refined beauties will be guided to the right choice.

We hope that this book will, like its predecessor, find its way onto the shelves of both the experienced fuchsia-grower and the beginner who is just starting to build a collection.

Miep Nijhuis

Fuchsias
arranged by colour

1   Alkmaars Glorie

2   Carla Johnson

3   Silver Dollar

4   Bergerac

5   Wiebke Becker

6   Delicate White

7   Montalba

8   St. Anne

9   Carefree

10   Igloo Maid

11   Squadron Leader

12   Torville and Dean

13   Bonsay

14   Constellation

15   Alyce Larson

16 Victorian

17 Ice Maiden

18 Nicky Veerman

19 Delta's Dream

20 Mötti

21 Keystone

22 Pink Most

23 Linda Copley

24 Monte Rosa

9

25 The Aristocrat

26 Robbie

27 Herjan de Groot

28 Linda Goulding

29 Hellas

30 De Groot's Beauty

31 Carmen Maria

32 Frau Margot Heinke

33 Crystal Blue

34 Alfred de Groot

35 Church Town

36 Waltzing Matilde

37 Ann Pacey

38 Royal and Ancient

39 Kay Riley

40 Romance

41 Rozientje

42 Whiteknight's Blush

43   Mia Goedman

44   Big Slim

45   Gwen Dodge

46   Lorna Swinbank

47   Gleneagles

48   Thamar

49   Misty Blue

50   Dutch Rosemarieke

51   Lican Ray

12

52   Ali Harder

53   Misty Haze

54   Olympic Lass

55   More Applause

56   Roesse Marie

57   Silver Dawn

58   Rayen

59   Fenman

60   Fairy Tales

61   Glowing Lilac

62   Mon Amie

63   Kit Oxtoby

64   Peppermint Candy

65   Joanne

66   Software

67   Win Oxtoby

68   Roesse Mondy

69   Montevideo

70   Pink Jade

71   Medalist

72   Trientje

73   Radings Mia

74   Bambini

75   Lütgerdina

76   Zaza

77   Walz Lucifer

78   Mollie Beaulah

79　Lee Antony

80　Reichards Sämling

81　Bled Lagon

82　Fransca

83　Pink Slippers

84　Heston Blue

85　Lindisfarne

86　Delta's Fair

87　Derby Star

88 Knights Errant

89 Dalli Dalli

90 Maresi

91 Mini

92 Piccolo

93 George Barr

94 Arels Zwaantje

95 Ken Jennings

96 Docteur Charles Favier

97   Rogier de Groot

98   Coachman Sämling

99   Taatje

100   Delta's Paljas

101   Waveney Gem

102   Roesse Wega

103   Roesse Willem

104   My Dear

105   Rose City

106   Belvedere

107   Crackerjack

108   Ajax

109   Hazel

110   Hilchenbacher Grusz

111   Adriaan

112   Jandel

113   Zolder's Glorie

114   Corsair

115   The Speedbird

116   Stella Marina

117   Television

118   Bloemelingen

119   Stad Ommen

120   Roland von Bremen

121   Crusader

122   Deep Purple

123   Turandot

124   Hans van de Beek

125   Anna Pauline

126   Hendrina Bovenschen

127   Tijl Uilenspiegel

128   City of Adelaïde

129   Diadem

130   Gordon's China Rose

131   Grusz an Graz

132   Florentina

21

133   Mabejo

134   Erika Frohmann

135   Lidi

136   Elisabeth Honorine

137   Woodnook

138   Hanau

139   Roesse Mieke

140   Steeley

141   Roesse Tricolor

142   Roesse Rowin

143   Humiko Kamo

144   Dawn Star

145   Ed Lagarde

146   Violetkoningin

147   Grimbeerd

148   Mina Knudde

149   Jaspers Groentje

150   Ostfriesland

151   Slippery Horn

152   Fleur de Picardie

153   Ati

154   Sinter Maarten

155   Lindsay Hendrickx

156   Task Force

157   Scarborough Starshine

158   Perry Park

159   Airdale

24

160   Pabbe's Blikoortje

161   Floretta

162   Kerry Ann

163   Koning Nobel

164   Lubbertje Hop

165   Max Jaffa

166   Wilson's Joy

167   Angela

168   Adriene Berger

169   Elisabeth Göring

170   Katie

171   Imperial Fantasy

172   Sweet Serenade

173   Danny Boy

174   Joe Kusber

175   La Fiesta

176   Jaspers Duimelot

177   Petit Four

178   Svenny

179   Berenvelt

180   Roesse Anja

181   Hans Peter Peters

182   Cap Arcona

183   Canada

184   Pride of the West

185   Cheers

186   Jan zonder Vrees

187   Roesse Femke

188   Playford

189   Frederike

190   Waveney Sunrise

191   Golden la Campanella

192   Elsine

193   Two Tiers

194   Jan van Maasakkers

195   Gerhard Mathieu

196   Panylla Prince

197   Little John

198   F. juntasensis

199   Lechlade Gorgon

200   Truus Gottmer

201   Charles de Gaulle

202   Cor Spek

203   Mrs. Susan Brookfield

204   Garden Boy

205   Sampson's Delight

206   Kentish Maid

207   Bubble Hanger

208   Buga '91

209   Flamenco Dancer

210   David Ward

211   Razzle Dazzle

212   Papa Bleuss

213   Jane Humber

214 English Rose

215 Danish Pastry

216 Lavender Kate

217 Ben Hur

218 Humboldt Holiday

219 Pale Flame

220 Topspin

221 Wapenvelds Bloei

222 Hölderlin

223 Long Distance

224 Jaspers Wentelwiek

225 Lilo Vogt

226 Daddy Longleg

227 Len Bielby

228 Pan

229 De Groot's Pipes

230 Delta's Prelude

231 Frozen Tears

232 Flor Izel

233 Walz Toorts

234 Gerburg Emmerich

235 George Johnson

236 Garden Week

237 Circe

238 Festival

239 Rakker

240 Subliem

33

241 Pieroy Liegois

242 Paulus

243 Joyce Sinton

244 Che Bella

245 Roesse Ministar

246 Nici's Findling

247 Ingelore

248 Erica Veldkamp

249 Ray Maslin

250   Sally Ann

251   Star Eyes

252   Tropicana

253   Bouvigne '91

254   Susan Green

255   Emile de Wildeman

256   R.A.F.

257   Beryl's Choice

258   Julia

259   Birgitt Heinke

260   Robin

261   Rocket Fire

262   Can Can

263   Ville de Liège

264   Bonita

265   Dulcie Elisabeth

266   Joop van Brakel

267   Joan Gilbert

268 Troubadour

269 Rose Aylett

270 Glockenspiel

271 Die Fledermaus

272 Kathy's Sparkler

273 Apache

274 Mallemolen

275 Palmengarten

276 Berba's Impossible

277   Pio Pico

278   Tosca

279   Merimbula Giant

280   Mama Bleuss

281   Bella Rosella

282   Silver Wings

283   Marty

284   Hilda

285   Anneke

286   Red Ace

287   Jeeves

288   Eden's Delight

289   Kathy Louise

290   Rosalie

291   Daniela

292   Mieke Meursing

293   Joan Leach

294   Jaspers Ringeling

295   Solmäs

296   Margaret Rose

297   Passing Cloud

298   Loch Lomond

299   Long John

300   Wieth

301   Haus Wiesengrund

302   Isle of Mull

303   Hercules

304　Delta's Delight

305　Frau Mint

306　Guurtje

307　Schildehof

308　Vicmarther

309　Monte Negro

310　Leodien

311　Jeanette Schwab

312　Walz Tuba

41

313   Walz Trompet

314   Walz Piano

315   Javelin

316   Janna

317   Jacqueline

318   Martien van Vugt

319   La Courneuve Fleury

320   Theseus

321   Geesche

322   Croix d'Honneur

323   President Elliot

324   Corallina

325   Soleil du Luxembourg

326   Tomma

327   Herzilein

328   Goldsworth Beauty

329   Doctor S.A. Appel

330   Lavaglut

331 Delta's Night   332 Driesje van den Berg   333 Eden Beauty

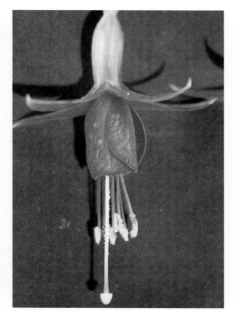

334 Huize Ruurlo   335 President   336 Rufus

337 Firenzi   338 Marloesje ter Beek   339 Les Hobbs

340   Alice Bayet

341   Joker

342   Walz Bugel

343   Lidie Bartelink

344   Geessien Not

345   Jaspers Vuurbal

346   Luscious

347   Geismar

348   Nuwenspete

349 Rose Phenomenal

350 Julicka

351 Comet

352 Daniel Lambert

353 Hendrina Josephina

354 Japmar Hofmeyer

355 Lottie Hobby

356 Corallina var. tricolori

357 Frau Hilde Rademacher

358   David

359   Petra de Groot

360   Roger Desiré

361   Hendrik den Besten

362   Lichtendorf

363   Golden Multa

364   Sulamith

365   Daniëlle Frijstein

366   Bas Weeda

367   Lotterer Queen

368   Karina

369   André le Nostre

370   Pluto

371   Profusion

372   Rieksken Boland

373   Gerharda's Aubergine

374   Grumpy

375   Martin's Leencor

376 Magilda

377 Janneke Brinkman-Salentijn

378 Joan's Delight

379 Banzai

380 Bertha Timmer

381 Liesbeth Jansen

382 Janna Roddenhof

383 Delta's Glorie

384 Delta's Drop

385   Königin der Frühe

386   Charming

387   Green 'n Gold

388   De Groot's Kruimel

389   Armand Simmon

390   Duke of York

391   Anna

392   Lilac Dainty

393   Sheila Crooks

50

394   Belle de Limbourg

395   Anna Marie

396   Westminster Chimes

397   Uranus

398   Robin Pacey

399   Italiano

400   Commander-in-Chief

401   Gracie

402   Parel van Waanrode

403   Ross Lea

404   Santa Paula

405   Victoria

406   Stientje Leget

407   Hermie Kainz

408   Renée

409   Jess

410   Sylvia Barker

411   Jülchen

412 Mrs. Marshall

413 Finn

414 Ebbtide

415 El Tope

416 Dennis

417 Delta's Symphonie

418 Delta's Song

419 Bettina

420 Violette Szabo

421   British Jubilee

422   Five Times

423   Gert Jan Bekamp

424   Jaap Brummel

425   De Groot's Robbedoes

426   Circus Spangles

427   Graf Spee

428   Deborah

429   Pabbe's Tudebekje

430   Marylin Olsen

431   Kyoto

432   Leine Perle

433   Herman de Graaff

434   Earrebarre

435   Liebelei

436   Madame Cornelissen

437   Gina

438   Stolze von Berlin

439   Centenary

440   Arcadia Gold

441   Kati

442   Schneewittchen

443   Hanna

444   Dolly Pausch

445   Alsace

446   Amie Josée Frans

447   Pink Quartette

448   Catharine Law

449   Wingrove's Mammoth

450   Sonata

451   Wilson's Pearls

452   Medusa

453   California Saga

454   New Fascination

455   De Groot's Lady

456   Citation

457 Delta's Memory

458 Martin's Yellow Surprise

459 F. fulgens variegata

460 Dutch Kingsize

461 Monty Python

462 Michel Schwab

463 Zet's Alpha

464 Golden Arrow

465 Insulinde

466   Brighton Belle

467   Engellina Schwab

468   Obergärtner Koch

469   F. fulgens var. rubra grandiflora
(met bont blad)

470   Ashley

471   Martin's Catharina

472   Sophie's Surprise

473   Oriental Sunrise

474   Katinka

475   Sophie Claire

476   Ken Goldsmith

477   Ymke

478   Jean

479   Jupiter Seventy

480   Mieke Alferink

481   Glitters

482   Ruddigor

483   Kim Broekhof

60

484   Golden Jubilee

485   Gelre

486   Danny Kaye

487   Orange Glow

488   Glowing Embers

489   Annie den Otter

490   Magic Flute

491   Eternal Flame

492   Dolly's Day Dream

493 Anita

494 Orangeblossom

495 Jacques Crasborn

496 Bolleken

497 Cyndy Robijn

498 Rebecca Williamson

499 Seventh Heaven

500 Born Free

Plant descriptions
arranged alphabetically

single:	4 or 5 petals	T	=	tube
semi-double:	5 to 7 petals	S	=	sepals
double:	8 or more petals	C	=	corolla

Numerals following the names refer to the colour illustrations on pages 7-62.

A

Adriaan 111
Double; T creamy-white with pink flush; S light pink, the upper side changing to light-green tips; underside light-pink with light yellow-green tip; C purplish-red, the outer petals with flamed orange-pink shades; large flower; very free-flowering; trailer; prefers filtered light.

Adriene Berger 168
Single; T creamy-pink with darker veins; S creamy-pink, at base paler, underside with pink flush, yellow-green tips; C purple-red, changing to violet-red, fading to orange-red, at base white, creamy-pink veins; medium-sized flower; free-flowering; upright grower; prefers filtered light.

Airdale 159
Semi-double; T white with greenish flush; S pale beetroot-red, towards the tips paler and changing to green; C medium beetroot-red; medium-sized flower; lax upright grower.

Ajax 108
Single; T glossy green; S very pale carmine-pink with ivory-white streak through the centre, at base slightly darker, underside pale-pink, small green tips; C violet-blue, at base pale-pink, red veins; rather large flower; free- and early flowering; self-branching; semi-trailer; prefers filtered light.

Alfred de Groot 34
Single; T vivid pink with darker veins; S pale phlox-pink, underneath darker, green tips; C violet-purple, at base white, pink veins with white spot along it; medium-sized saucer-shaped flower; free-flowering; semi-trailer; suitable for a climber.

Ali Harder 52
Single; T white tinted pink; S white, at base pale-pink flush, large green tips; C bright lilac, at base white; small flower; very free-flowering; self-branching; upright grower; for filtered light; suitable for standards.

Alice Bayet 340
Semi-double; T palest crimson; S pale crimson with small greenish-white tips; C deep beetroot-red; rather large flower; free-flowering; trailer.

Alkmaars Glorie 1
Single; T pink, white striped; S very light yellow-green, at tips slightly darker; C white; rather large well-shaped flower; trailer.

Alsace 445
Double; T crimson with darker grooves; S carmine-red with green tips; C carmine-red, at base white with carmine, pink-tinted; rather large flower; free-flowering; self-branching; upright grower; suitable for full sun.

Alyce Larson 15
Double; R ivory-white; S white; C white, at base slighly pink, pink veins; large flower; free-flowering; trailer; doesn't like rain, wind and heat; not suitable for sun; best for a sheltered place in a container.

Amie Josée Frans 446
Double; T rose-red; S rose-red tinted with white and pink, green tips; C white, at base slightly pink; large full flower; free-flowering; self-branching; upright grower; suitable for full sun.

André le Nostre 369
Double; T bright carmine-red; S bright carmine-red, underside with orange glow; C purple-blue, fading to violet, at base carmine-red, darker edges, underside orange, crimson veins and splashes; petaloïds are violet-purple with orange base; large flower; self-branching; tall upright grower with long horizontal branches.

Angela 167
Double; T palest pink; S palest pink with small green tips; C bright violet-pink; medium-sized flower; trailer.

Anita 493
Single; T white; S creamy-white with green tips; C salmon-orange, at base slightly lighter; upright grower.

Ann Pacey 37
Semi-double; T white with pink grooves; S greenish white, at base grown together, green tips; C pale pink, at base green-white; rather large flower; very free- and early flowering; self-branching; upright grower; best grown in shade; suitable for training as a standard.

Anna 391
Double; T bright red; S bright red; C magenta, at base red, faint red veins; large flower; upright grower; suitable for full sun.

Anna Marie 395
Double; T scarlet-red; S scarlet-red; C violet, changing to lighter violet, at base carmine-pink and carmine-pink veins, many petaloïds violet with carmine-pink splashes; full rather large flower; free-flowering; branches well; trailer; best colour in filtered light.

Anna Pauline 125
Semi-double; T glossy ivory-white with green flush; S ivory-white, on the underside tinted violet; C violet maturing to purple, at base pink, violet veins with pale violet splash; rather large flower; very free-flowering; for filtered light.

Anneke 285
Double; T carmine-pink with darker veins; S carmine-pink with lighter tips; C bluish-violet maturing to violet-purple, at base pale-pink; rather large flower; trailer.

Annie den Otter 489
Single; T appleblossom-pink; S upper side mandarin-red, underside pale mandarin-red, green tips; C bright carmine-pink, at base pale orange; rather large flower; free-flowering; self-branching; upright grower; suitable for training as a standard and pillar; for full sun.

Apache 273
Double; T carmine-red; S carmine-red, small green tips; C lilac, at base carmine-red, carmine veins; medium-sized flower; free-flowering; self-branching; semi-trailer; for filtered light.

Arcadia Gold 440
Double; T cerise-red with darker veins; S dull cerise-red, small green tips; C ivory-white, carmine-red veins; medium-sized flower; free-flowering; variegated light green foliage with cream edges; semi-trailer; for full sun; needs a lot of pinching for sufficient quantity of bloom.

Arels Zwaantje 94
Single; T waxy-white with green faint; S waxy-white with deep-pink blush, small green tips; C purple-lilac with pink veins, at base white; fairly large flower; free-flowering; self-branching; trailer; for filtered light.

Armand Simmon 389
Double; T waxy currant-red; S upper side waxy-currant-red, underside bright wine-red; C bright violet, fading to dull-violet, at base red, sharp red veins with coral-pink splashes along it; full rather large flower; free-flowering somewhat late; beautiful yellow-green foliage with red pedicel and veins; upright grower; suitable for full sun; flower as beautiful red flower-stalk.

Asley 470
Single; T from base fading from dark-red to somewhat lighter red; S on the upper side red, changing to a brown tip, on the underside orange-red changing to a yellow-green tip; C pale orange-red, at base darker and darker veins; medium-sized, long slender flower; upright grower; needs shade.

Ati 153
Single; T white with spiraea-pink flush and purple veins; S upper side spiraea-pink with darker edges, underside orchid-pink, long olive-green tips; C bright robin-red with darker edges and veins; long slender flower; trailer; needs a shady place; triphylla-type.

B

Bambini 74
Single; T reddish-pink; S reddish-pink; C lilac-mauve, at base pink and pink veins; small flower held out; free-flowering; upright bushy grower; dwarf.

Banzai 379
Single; T glossy robin-red; S robin-red, on underside purple, green tips; C robin-red with slightly darker veins; fairly small flower; upright grower; for filtered light.

Bas Weeda 366
Single; T crimson; S crimson with lighter tips; C crimson; medium-sized flower; bushy grower; requires a shady place.

Bella Rosella 281
Double; T waxy-white with green faint and stripes; S waxy-white with pink faint; C dark-violet, fading to purple, at base pink, red veins with pink splash along it; large flossy flower; very floriferous; self-branching; trailer; requires filtered light and a sheltered place.

Belle de Limbourg 394
Single; T pale-red; S upper side bright red, tips somewhat darker, underside red, bluish glow; C purple-violet, at base carmine-red, red veins with rose-red splash; upright grower.

Belvedere 106
Double; T white with green; S white, at tips green; C blue-violet, at base lighter, many petaloïds; large flower; lax upright grower.

Ben Hur 217
Double; T coral-pink; S coral-pink; C purple with pink and white splashes; very large flower; trailer.

Berba's Impossible 276
Semi-double; T pink; S pink; C lilac-blue with pink splashes, at base pale-pink, the outer petals with many pink splashes; large flossy flower; very free-flowering; semi-trailer; for full sun.

Berenvelt 179
Single; T rose-red; S soft rose-red with small green tips; C bluish rose-red; medium-sized flower with long tube; trailer.

Bergerac 4
Single; T white; S on upper side white with pink stripes, underneath white with pink flush at base, green tips; C ivory-white, at base pink blush; fairly large flower; free-flowering; self-branching; semi-trailer; requires filtered light conditions.

Bertha Timmer 380
Single; T aubergine-purple with darker stripes; S aubergine-purple with yellow-green tips; C dark aubergine-purple; small flower; upright grower; requires a shady location.

Beryl's Choice 257
Double; T pale-pink with darker grooves; S pink with darker stripes fading into white towards the tips, underside deep-pink, green tips; C light violet with pink splashes, at base pink, dark-pink veins; large flower; branches with difficulty; upright grower; needs a sheltered place and dislikes rain, wind, sun and heat.

Bettina 419
Single; T waxy-white with darker veins, S white with a touch of pink, green tips; C purple, at base pink, darker edges; fairly small flower; very floriferous; self-branching; semi-trailer; plant with stiff branches; for filtered light.

Big Slim 44
Single; T pink with darker veins; S upper side pink with deep-pink edge, underside slightly darker, bright-green tip; C candy-pink, at base orange-red, smoky glow; very long slender flower; trailer; tolerant of full sun.

Birgitt Heinke 259
Double; T rose-red; S rose-red, yellow-green, small tips; C bright purple-blue, at base pink; large flossy flower; very free-flowering; self-branching; upright grower; for full sun; suitable to train as a standard or pillar.

Bled Lagon 81
Double; T white; S white; C rose-red, with large lighter pink splashes from the base; large flower; lax upright grower; can also be trained as a trailer.

Bloemelingen 118
Double; T greenish-white; S upper side greenish-white, underside soft purple-pink, changing to white towards the tips; C blue-violet, at base somewhat lighter; large flower; upright grower.

Bolleken 496
Double; T white with touch of green; S white with touch of green and yellow-green tips; C flesh-coloured pink; large full flower; lax upright grower.

Bonita 264
Double; T pale-pink; S pink with green tips; C purple-pink, at base pale-pink splashes, red veins; large flower; reasonable flowering; self-branching; trailer; strong plant.

Bonsay 13
Double; T ivory-white with green flush; S ivory-white with green tips; C ivory-white; fairly large flower; lax upright grower.

Born Free 500
Double; T creamy-white; S creamy-white; C carmine-red, at base white; medium-sized flower; trailer.

Bouvigne '91 253
Semi-double; T red; S red with green tips; C blue-purple, fading to pink, at base red, purple edges; many petaloïds; large flower; free-flowering, flowers early and long-lasting; strong upright grower; needs careful pinching; for filtered light.

Brighton Belle 466
Single; T rose-red with darker stripes; S salmon-pink, underside orange-pink, salmon-pink tips; C salmon-orange, at base orange, pink-orange edges and orange veins; long slender flower; very floriferous, early in bloom and long-lasting; self-branching; foliage with red pedicel and veins; upright grower; sun-tolerant; triphylla-type.

British Jubilee 421
Double; T waxy-white, long and slender; S upper side waxy-white with pink glow, underside waxy-white with salmon-pink blush, very large bright green tips; C the four central petals are carmine-red, the others are strawberry-red, at base pale pink, strawberry-red veins, the petaloïds pale strawberry-red; large full flower; free-flowering and long-lasting; lax grower, suitable for baskets; sun-tolerant.

Bubble Hanger 207
Single; T rose-madder; S pale rose-madder, underside slightly darker; C lilac-pink, at base somewhat lighter; fairly large flower; free-flowering; self-branching; trailer; requires a sheltered site, dislikes rain, wind and sun.

Buga '91 208
Semi-double; T carmine-pink with carmine-pink stripes; S carmine-pink, underside carmine-red, green tips; C lilac-violet, at base pale pink, carmine-pink veins with pale-pink splash; medium-sized flower; very free-flowering; self-branching; upright grower; beautiful red branches.

C

California Saga 453
Single; T salmon-orange; S pale scarlet-red, becoming paler towards the tips, underside vermilion-red, green tips; C signal-red, at base orange-red, edges somewhat deeper red, faint veins; large flower; upright grower; can be grown as a standard; sun-tolerant; strong fuchsia with beautiful buds.

Can Can 262
Semi-double; T rose-red with darker stripes; S rose-red, small green tips; C lilac-pink, aging to cyclamen-purple, at base crimson, crimson veins with violet splash along it; large flower; free-flowering; self-branching; upright grower; for filtered light.

Canada 183
Double; T rose-red with white veins; S rose-red, on the underside pink, green tips; C purple-red, maturing to red, at base pink, red veins and pink splashes, purple-red glow; fairly large flower; trailer; dislikes rain, wind, heat and sun; suitable for containers.

Cap Arcona 183
Semi-double; T vivid candy-pink with darker grooves; S vivid candy-pink at base changing to white at the tips; C violet-blue; medium-sized flower; free-flowering; upright grower.

Carefree 9
Double; T white with green stripes; S white with faint pink and green veins, green tips; C white with touch of pink, maturing to pink, at base with pink splashes, pale carmine-red veins; medium-sized flower; free-flowering; trailer; requires a sheltered site; splendid fuchsia!

Carla Johnson 2
Single; T ivory-white with pink blush and green stripes; S greenish-white with pink blush, a red stripe from base along the edges, underside white with pink blush, green tips; C white, lilac veins, lilac glow; medium-sized flower held out; very free-flowering; self-branching; upright bushy grower; tolerates full sun.

Carmen Maria 31
Single; T pink with dark-pink stripes; S upper side pale pink, underside slightly darker pink, green tips; C pale-pink with somewhat darker pink veins; medium-sized flower; free-flowering; self-branching; lax bushy grower or trailer; likes a sheltered site.

Catharine Law 448
Double; T rose-red; S rose-red, green tips; C white, at base rose-red; rather large flower; upright grower.

Centenary 439
Double; T crimson; S crimson; C phlox-purple, at base red, red veins, carmine-red splashes, medium-sized flower; free-flowering; self-branching; upright bushy grower.

Charles de Gaulle 201
Single; T deep-pink; S deep-pink, on the tips green; S deep-pink, at base slightly lighter; long slender flower.

Charming 386
Single; T rose-red; S glossy rose-red; C purple, maturing to red-purple, at base rose-red; medium-sized flower; very floriferous; self-branching; upright grower; lovely yellow-green foliage; easy to grow.

Che Bella 244
Single; T pale-pink; S pink, underneath slightly darker, yellow tips; C cerise-red with faint pink veins; fairly large flower held out; trailer; dislikes rain and heat; suitable for growing in containers.

Cheers 185
Double; T pale-pink with darker veins; S upper side deep-pink with grooves and pale splashes, underside paler pink, at base orange, pale-pink tips; C cyclamen-red, at base orange splashes, darker red edges; large flower; self-branching; tall upright grower; difficult to grow to a good shape, dislikes wind.

Church Town 35
Semi-double; T palest pink; S palest pink with small green tips; C rose-purple, at base lighter; medium-sized flower; upright grower.

Circe 237
Semi-double; T pale strawberry-red with green stripes; S pale strawberry-red, green tips; C violet-blue, maturing to violet-purple, at base pale pink, red veins; medium-sized flower; free-flowering; semi-trailer.

Circus Spangles 426
Double; T white; S white, underside pale-pink; C rose-red, at base white, rather large flower; trailer.

Citation 456
Single; T rose-red with green tips; C white with at base rose-red veins; fairly large flower; free-flowering; self-branching; upright grower; dislikes rain, wind, sun and heat; prone to botrytis.

City of Adelaide 128
Double; T greenish-white with pink blush and green stripes; S white with pink blush at base, red edges, underside mauve, green tips; C fairly dark violet, fading to purple-violet, at base white, red veins with white splashes along it; medium-sized flower; free-flowering; tall upright grower with stiff branches; requires filtered light.

Coachman Sämling 98
Single; T creamy-white, underneath pale-violet; C violet, at base slightly lighter; medium-sized flower; trailer.

Comet 351
Semi-double; T cerise-red with darker veins; S cerise-red with darker veins and green tips; C blue-purple, at base red splashes, red veins, silvery glow; large flower; reasonable flowering; tall upright grower.

Commander-in-Chief 400
Double; T deep rose-red; S upper side crimson, fading to carmine-red, underside crimson, at base deep rose-red with orange glow, pale-green tips; C fuchsia-purple fading to violet, at base deep rose-red, reddish edges, dark-red veins with deep-rose-red splashes along it, the petaloids are fuchsia-purple with fancy rose-red splashes; large compact flower held out; free-flowering; branches reasonable; tall upright grower; bush for full sun; strong plant.

Constellation 14
Double; T white with green veins; S white, underneath with green veins, green tips; C white with pink veins; fairly large flower; early flowering; upright grower; intolerant of sun and heat; requires a sheltered place; prone to botrytis.

Cor Spek 202
Single; T pale fuchsia-red; S upper side pale fuchsia-red, underside Bengal pink; C purple; medium-sized flower with long tube; free-flowering; upright grower; resistant for full sun

Corallina 324
Single; T carmine-red; S carmine-red; C dark-purple, at base red, red veins; medium-sized flower; free-flowering; self-branching with horizontal spreading branches; rather small foliage with red veins and stem; upright grower, can be grown as a semi-trailer; doesn't like wind, sun and heat; requires a sheltered condition.

Corallina var. tricolori 356
Single; T rose-red to scarlet-red; S rose-red to scarlet-red, underside slightly lighter; C purple-blue, at base pink, purple veins, from base a decreasing pink splash; medium-sized slender flower; reasonable and late flowering; lovely cream, green and rose-red foliage; trailer or lax grower.

Corsair 114
Double; T white with touch of green, and green grooves at base; S white with green tips, underside white with touch of pink; C the inner petals are white, other petals are dark lavender-blue to purple with white at base, the outer ones are white with purple marbled with pink; large flower; branches slowly; lax grower, semi-trailer; dislikes wind, sun and heat, requires a sheltered condition; needs a lot of pinching.

Crackerjack 107
Single/semi-double; T greenish-white with pink faint; S white with pale-pink blush, underneath slightly darker; C dark-mauve, at base white, pink veins; large flower; very free-flowering; self-branching; trailer; requires a sheltered and shady site.

Croix d'Honneur 322
Single; T bright cardinal-red; S cardinal-red, paler tips; C pale aubergine, at base somewhat lighter; long slender flower; upright compact grower; can be grown as a trailer and as a bush; requires filtered light.

Crusader 121
Double; T white with pink flush; S white with pink flush and green tips; C deep-purple, at base white splash, white veins, red flush; rather large flower; trailer or semi-trailer; requires a sheltered place; suitable for containers.

Crystal Blue 33
Double; T white with green grooves; S white with green veins and pink flush, on the underside pink; C lilac, at base white splash; large flower; normal flowering; trailer; requires a sheltered site; suitable for grown in containers.

Cyndy Robijn 497
Double; T white-pink with pink stripes; S soft-pink with green tips; C violet-pink, fading to greyish-pink, paler at base, reddish veins; large flower; trailer.

D

Daddy Longleg 226
Single; T rose-red; S rose-red; C pink-orange; long slender flower; semi-trailer.

Dalli Dalli 89
Single; T glossy ivory-white; S ivory-white, underside with green stripe, green tips; C violet-purple, fading to purple, at base ivory-white with green flush, darker edges, greenish veins with pink splash along it; small flower; free-flowering; upright grower; can be trained as a semi-trailer; for filtered light.

Daniel Lambert 352
Single; T cerise-red; S cerise-red; C mauve, at base pink; medium-sized bell-shaped flower; free-flowering; upright grower; can be grown as a standard.

Daniela 291
Single; T vivid purple-pink; S vivid purple-pink; C pale lilac-pink, at base red, red veins and pink splash; small flower; very floriferous; self-branching; upright grower; dwarf; suitable for a small bush; requires filtered light.

Daniëlle Frijstein 365
Single; T glossy red; S upper side glossy red, underside red; C red-purple, at base somewhat lighter; fairly small flower; very floriferous; early flowering and long-lasting; self-branching; trailer; dwarf; easy to grow.

Danish Pastry 215
Single; T greenish white with a touch of pink; S pale coral-pink, underside coral-pink with white splashes, green tips; C lavender-blue, fading to coral-pink, at base salmon-pink, salmon-pink splashes; large flower; very free-flowering; self-branching; trailer; needs a sheltered site.

Danny Boy 173
Double; T pale coral-red; S pale coral-red with green tips; C dark rose-red, at base rose, red edges; very large flower; reasonable and late flowering; upright lax grower; can be best trained as a trailer; not an easy one.

Danny Kay 486
Double; T pink with green stripes; S upper side soft-red to the tips shading to green, underside slightly lighter; C dark orange-red, at base pale soft-red; medium-sized flower; upright grower; can well be grown as trailer.

David 358
Single; T glossy tomato-red; S glossy tomato-red; C dark-purple; fairly small flower; self-branching; lax upright grower.

David Ward 210
Double; T white; S upper side white, on the underside with purple blush; C violet-purple, at base lighter; medium-sized flower; upright grower.

Dawn Star 144
Double; T white with green grooves and pink flush; S greenish-white, at base a touch of pink, underside greenish-white, green tips; C blue-purple, fading to lilac-purple, at base pink, faint pink veins; rather large flower; very floriferous; self-branching; upright grower; for a sheltered place in filtered light; needs careful pinching.

De Groot's Beauty 30
Single/semi-double; T white shading to shell-pink; S orchid-pink shading to pale pink, bright fuchsia-purple edges, on the underside bright fuchsia-purple with green tips; C lavender-pink with fuchsia-purple veins; medium-sized flower; lax grower; suitable to be trained as semi-trailer; tolerates full sun.

De Groot's Lady 455
Single; T pale shell-pink with green flush and green stripes; S upper side at base white with cyclamen-pink blush, large vivid green tip, the underside cherry-pink; C white, cherry-pink at base; rather large flower; upright grower; tolerates full sun and heat; suitable for training as a standard.

De Groot's Kruimel 388
Double; T cardinal-red; S cardinal-red on the upper side, underside carmine-red; C robin-red; rather large flower; free-flowering; trailer; said to be hardy.

De Groot's Pipes 229
Single; T at the base shell-pink fading to orchid-pink, bright robin-red stripes; S at the base bright robin-red, to the tip orchid-pink, olive-green tips, on the underside bright light robin-pink; C deep robin-red; medium-sized flower; trailer; requires filtered light.

De Groot's Robbedoes 425
Single; T white with a touch of green and darker stripes; S upper side white with a touch of pink, underside pink-scarlet, large green tips; C candy-pink with darker edges and veins, at base palest pink; medium-sized flower; early flowering; trailer; suitable for full sun.

Deborah 428
Double; T white with pink blush and red stripes; S greenish-white with a touch of pink and darker grooves, underside white, green tips; C pale reddish-purple fading to dull purple, orange flush, orange at base, pale purple edge, irregular white, sometimes orange splashes, many petaloids; large flower; very floriferous; self-branching; trailer; bushy grower; suitable for baskets; needs a sheltered site protected from wind and rain.

Deep Purple 122
Double; T white with pink glow; S white with pink flush, green tips; C violet-blue; rather large flower; semi-trailer.

Delicate White 6
Single; T white with green faint; S on the upper side from base white shading to phlox-pink, underside white shading to phlox-pink, green tips; C transparent white with pale-pink veins; medium-sized flower; upright grower; needs a place in filtered light.

Delta's Delight 304
Single; T pink; S pink, upper side with darker veins, underside pink, small white to pale-green tips; C violet with darker veins; rather small flower; semi-trailer; sun-tolerant.

Delta's Dream 19
Single; T white with grey-green flush; S white with grey-green flush; C pale shell-pink with darker veins and purple-pink edges; fairly small flower; upright grower; lovely, delicate colour-combination.

Delta's Drop 384
Single; T crimson with darker stripes; S crimson; C dull-purple fading to beetroot-red, crimson splash on base, the petals with clear stems; medium-sized flower; upright grower; needs a shaded place.

Delta's Fair 86
Single; T white with green flush; S white with green flush, underside white with purple blush, green tip; C deep-lilac, at base white; medium-sized flower held out somewhat; free-flowering; trailer; requires a sheltered site; also known as Delta's Fleur.

Delta's Glorie 383
Single; T red-aubergine spotted; S somewhat lighter red-aubergine; C purple-aubergine; medium-sized flower; very floriferous and long-lasting; branches well; upright grower; tolerates full sun.

Delta's Memory 457
Single; T rose-red; S pale aubergine-red with darker veins; C white-pink with obvious aubergine-coloured veins; rather large flower; flowers over long period; upright grower; needs careful pinching; requires a sheltered position.

Delta's Night 331
Single; T deep red-purple, rather long; S deep red-purple, on the tips lighter, small green tips; C deep-purple, near black; rather large flower; upright grower; sun-tolerant; well-shaped flower.

Delta's Paljas 100
Single; T white with appleblossom-pink blush; S pale appleblossom-pink, on the underside pink; C fuchsia-purple to dark ' robin-red; medium-sized flower; semi-trailer; requires shade.

Delta's Prelude 230
Single; T dull carmine-pink; S upper side pale fuchsia-red, underside slightly darker, small green tips; C bright robin-red, petals have small stems; medium-sized flower; free-flowering; trailer; for full sun.

Delta's Song 418
Single; T white; S upper side white with carmine-pink faint, underside carmine-pink; C vivid rose-red changing to cardinal-red; medium-sized flower; upright grower; for full sun.

Delta's Symphonie 417
Double; T yellow/greenish-white; S pale purple-pink, yellow-green tips, underside pale purple-red, changing to darker tips; C dark red-purple; medium-sized flower; upright grower; needs a sheltered place.

Dennis 416
Single; T white with rose-red blush and rose-red stripes; S white with small green tips, at base rose-red; C deep robin-red, with orange glow at base; medium-sized flower; upright grower.

Derby Star 87
Single; T white with grey-pink blush; S white with grey-pink blush and green tips; C purple-blue and violet-blue spotted; medium-sized flower; free-flowering; upright grower.

Diadem 129
Double; T white with yellow-greenish faint; S white, underside white with touch of purple-pink; small green tips; C blue-violet with pink splashes, fading to magenta, at base pink, pink veins with whitish-pink splash along it; rather large flower; free-flowering; upright grower; requires filtered light; can be grown as a standard; very striking fuchsia.

Die Fledermaus 271
Double; T scarlet-red; S scarlet-red; C blue-violet with at base pale-pink splashes, rose-red veins; fairly large flower; self-branching; semi-trailer; strong plant.

Docteur Charles Favier 96
Single; T white with purple-pink blush; S upper side white with purple-pink blush, underside pale purple-pink; C vivid purple-pink, at base white; medium-sized flower; trailer.

Doctor S.A. Appel 329
Single; T bright red; S bright red, underside slightly lighter; C very deep purple, at base pale-pink and deep-purple edges, velvet glow; rather small flower; very free and early flowering; self-branching; upright grower.

Dolly Pausch 444
Double; T glossy rose-red; S glossy rose-red; C ivory-white with on base red veins; large full flower; lax upright grower; can be grown as semi-trailer; strong grower.

Dolly's Day Dream 492
Double; T white with pink blush; S white with pink blush, green tips; C orange-pink; medium-sized flower; semi-trailer.

Driesje van den Berg 332
Single; T glossy deep-purple, ball-shaped; S deep-purple; C deep-robin-red; medium-sized flower; tall upright grower; needs filtered light and shade.

Duke of York 390
Single; T glossy pale-red; S glossy pale-red, dull red tips; C blue-purple, at base somewhat red; fairly small flower; free-flowering; self-branching; upright bushy grower; lovely variegated yellow-green foliage with red veins and steel; suitable for containers.

Dulcie Elisabeth 265
Double; T rose-red; S rose-red; C blue with pale- and deep-pink splashes and deep-pink veins, at base pink; rather large flower; free-flowering; self-branching; upright grower; suitable for containers.

Dutch Kingsize 460
Single; T pale yellow-orange; S upper side pale-orange changing to yellow-green, underside pale orange-red; C pale orange-red; very long slender flower; tall upright grower; needs careful and frequent pinching; requires a sheltered and warm position.

Dutch Rosemarieke 50
Single; T greenish-white with pink blush and green stripes; S white with green tips, on the underside pale-pink; C soft violet-purple changing to lavender-pink, at base green, cyclamen-pink edges, pale red veins; medium-sized flower; very floriferous; self-branching; upright grower; for filtered light.

Earrebarre 434
Single; T aubergine-red; S aubergine-red; C white with aubergine veins and at base aubergine-red; medium-sized flower; early- and free-flowering; self-branching; upright bushy grower; requires filtered light.

Ebbtide 414
Double; T white with pale pink blush; S upper side white, underside pale pink, green tips; C purple-blue, fading to red-purple, at base pink, velvet glow; large flossy flower; early flowering; vigorous trailer; requires cool sheltered site.

Ed Lagarde 145
Double; T white; S white, underside with pink flush, green tips; C purple-blue, at base white, pink veins; large flower; trailer; dislikes rain, wind, sun and heat; needs sheltered conditions.

Eden Beauty 333
Single; T crimson; S crimson, underside rose-red, pale-green tips; C cyclamen-purple, fading to violet-purple, at base rose-red, red edges; fairly large flower; free-flowering; self-branching; bushy-growing trailer; sun-tolerant.

Eden's Delight 288
Single; T greenish-white with red blush and green stripes; S upper side carmine-red, changing to carmine-pink, underside bright carmine-red, green tips; C pale violet with darker edges and striking red veins; medium-sized flower held out; very floriferous; bushy upright grower; can be grown as a standard; for full sun.

El Tope 415
Single; T waxy-white with green faint, carmine-pink at base and carmine-pink veins; S waxy-white, on the tips green, small carmine-red edge; C deep robin-red, at base a touch white, darker veins with white splash along it; rather large flower; well-flowering; self-branching; stiff upright grower; for filtered light; can be trained as a pillar.

Elisabeth Göring 169
Single; T white with a touch of pink and pink stripes; S white, narrow pink edge at base, underside white with pink blush, large pale-green tips; C purple-blue, at base carmine-pink, red veins with carmine-pink splash; medium-sized flower; very floriferous; lax upright grower or semi-trailer; for filtered light; suitable for training as a standard or small pillar.

Elisabeth Honirine 136
Single; T white with green glow; S white, underside with a touch pink; C deep purple-violet with a tinge of petunia-purple; medium-sized flower; semi-trailer; requires shade.

Elsine 192
Single; T pink with darker stripes; S phlox-pink with darker stripes, underside pink-purple with darker stripes, small green tips; C bright violet-purple, at the base slightly lighter, darker veins; fairly small flower held out; free-flowering; needs careful pinching; lovely fuchsia with beautiful flower shape and unusual combination of colours.

Emile de Wildeman 255
Double; T carmine-red with darker grooves; S carmine-red; C deep-pink fading to blush-pink, at base carmine-red, cerise-red veins, from base carmine-red splashes; rather large flower; free-flowering; self-branching; upright grower; easy fuchsia to grow.

Engellina Schwab 467
Single; T orange-red; S orange with brown-red tips; C orange; long slender flower; upright grower; suitable for full sun.

English Rose 214
Double; T white; S white with green tips; C deep lavender-purple; large flower; reasonable flowering; upright bushy grower; lovely flower with beautiful colour.

Erica Veldkamp 248
Double; T pink with darker stripes; S upper side pale carmine-pink, underside pale scarlet-red; C blood-red; medium-sized flower; lax grower; can be grown as semi-trailer.

Erika Frohmann 134
Double; T yellow-green; S white with green tips; C purple-blue with pink splashes; rather large flower; semi-trailer.

Eternal Flame 491
Semi-double; T salmon-pink; S salmon-pink, underside paler, green tips; C smoky pink with orange veins, at base salmon-pink, darker edges; medium-sized flower; reasonable and late flowering; upright lax grower; dislikes rain, wind, sun and heat.

F. fulgens variegata 459
Single; T and S pink-orange; C pink-orange; long slender flower; variegated foliage; species.

F. fulgens var. rubra grandiflora (with variegated foliage) 469
Single; T and S pale red; C bright red; long slender flower; flowers in terminal racemes; variegated foliage; bush does not turn woody, species.

F. juntasensis 198
Single; T pink-purple with dark purple grooves; S pale pink, underside greenish; there are no petals; vigorous bush; large velvet foliage; species.

Fairy Tales 59
Semi-double; T dull rose-red with carmine-red stripes; S pale pink, underside pale-candy-pink with stripes, pale-green tips; C pink, at base deeper coloured, lilac tinge; medium-sized flower; free-flowering; trailer; suitable for full sun; beautiful buds.

Fenman 59
Single; T carmine-pink with darker stripes; S pale pink, underside cherry-pink, green tips; C soft-pink, at base pink, cherry-pink veins; medium-sized flower; free-flowering; branches well; upright grower with stiff branches; for full sun.

Festival 238
Double; T salmon-pink with darker stripes; S salmon-pink to the tips changing to white, underside pink, green tips; C red-purple, at base scarlet-red, darker veins; medium-sized flower; upright grower.

Finn 413
Single; T ivory-white; S ivory-white with pink tinge and green tips; C smoky dark-pink to purple, at base white, bluish glow; medium-sized flower; free-flowering; semi-trailer; very unusual-coloured bloom.

Firenzi 337
Single; T robin-red; S robin-red; C crimson; medium-sized flower; upright grower.

Five Times 422
Single; T white; S pale pink-orange; C strawberry-red; medium-sized flower; upright grower.

Flamenco Dancer 209
Double; T soft purple-pink; S upper side soft purple-pink, on the underside purple-pink; C splashed violet and rather dark purple-pink; fairly large flower; trailer.

Fleur de Picardie 152
Single; T pale pink with darker stripes; S upper side pale pink, underside cyclamen-pink, pale-green tips; C purple-violet, deep purple-violet edges; long slender flower with very long tube; upright grower; suitable for growing as a standard; likes a site in filtered light.

Flor Izel 232
Double; T soft rose-red; S soft rose-red with darker blush; C crimson, at base lighter; medium-sized flower; free-flowering; self-branching; trailer; tolerates full sun and heat.

Florentina 132
Double; T greenish-white; S clear white with green tips; C smoky wine-red, fading to red, at the base orange-pink, orange-pink splashes; large full flower; semi-trailer; requires a sheltered place in filtered light; lovely fuchsia with unusual combination of colour.

Floretta 161
Single; T white with green stripes and pink blush; S white with carmine-red blush, pale-green tips; C fuchsia-purple, fading to robin-red, at the base pink, darker edges and veins; rather small flower; free-flowering; self-branching; upright bushy grower; for filtered light.

Fransca 82
Single; T white with pink stripes, green tinge; S white with green tinge, green tips; C blue-violet, at base white with blue-violet blush, red veins and pale-pink splash; fairly small flower; self-branching; trailer; for filtered light.

Frau Hilde Rademacher 357
Double; T glossy bright red; S glossy bright red, underneath carmine-red; C blue-violet, at base salmon-pink, purple-blue edge, red veins and salmon-pink to cerise-red splashes; medium-sized flower held out somewhat; free-flowering; branches well; upright, somewhat lax grower; takes full sun.

Frau Margot Heinke 32
Semi-double/double; T white with green tinge and green stripes; S upper side white with green tinge, underside cherry-pink with green-white streak through the centre; large green tips; C purple-pink with red veins; rather large, somewhat loose flower; very floriferous; self-branching; bushy-growing semi-trailer; for full sun.

Frau Mint 305
Single; T pink with greenish tinge; S upper side pink; underside darker; C blue-purple, fading to violet-purple, at base paler; medium-sized flower; lax upright grower; can be grown as a trailer or for containers.

Frederike 189
Semi-double; T glossy greenish-white with pink grooves; S white with pink blush and pink grooves, underside carmine-pink, green tips; C purple-violet, at the base salmon-pink, darker edge, from base orange splashes; rather large flower; free-flowering; branches well; upright grower; does best in shade.

Frozen Tears 231
Single/semi-double; T pale-red; S upper side dark-red with blue glow, underside red; yellow-green tips; C red-purple, at base crimson; rather large flower; very floriferous; self-branching; trailer; needs filtered light.

Garden Boy 204
Double; T white with pink and greenish blush; S pale pink, underside darker pink; C deep-purple-violet, at base changing to red-violet; medium-sized flower; trailer.

Garden Week 236
Double; T pale-pink with green tinge and darker stripes; S white with pink blush on the upper side, underside carmine-red, green tips; C purple-red to purple-violet, at the base salmon-pink with white splash, red veins, fancy pale carmine-red splashes; large flower; reasonable flowering; semi-trailer; difficult to train into a good shape; needs a sheltered position in filtered light.

Geesche 321
Single; T bright rose-red with bright pink blush and darker veins; S upper side carmine-red to carmine-pink; underside carmine-red; small green tips; C purple-mauve, at base vivid rose-red, bluish edge, red veins and vivid rose-red splash; medium-sized flower held out; very floriferous; upright, stiff grower; suitable for full sun.

Geessien Not 344
Single; T glossy bright red with darker stripes; S upper side cerise-red with darker veins, underside vivid cerise-red; C deep-purple with cerise-red veins; small flower held out; very floriferous; self-branching; bushy grower; requires a sheltered condition.

Geismar 347
Single; T pale-pink with greenish tinge and darker veins; S upper side carmine-red with darker veins, underside crimson, green tips; C pale pink, at base carmine-red, red veins and orchid-pink splash, pale lilac tinge; medium-sized flower; very floriferous; self-branching; upright grower with horizontal branches; long internodes; suitable to grow as a pyramid; takes full sun and bright light.

Gelre 485
Semi-double; T cream with orange glow; S pale carmine-pink; C crimson, at base pale carmine-pink, darker edges; rather large flower; very floriferous; semi-trailer; can be grown as a trailer; for full sun.

George Barr 93
Single; T white with pink blush; S white with on the base pink, fading to pink, green tips, very long sepals; C violet-blue fading to violet-purple, at base purple, purple edge, pink veins; fairly small flower; very floriferous; self-branching; upright bushy grower; suitable to grow as a standard.

George Johnson 235
Single; T rose-red; S pale rose-red, underside slightly darker; C rose-red-purple, fading to paler violet, at base pale pink, pale-red veins; medium-sized flower; upright bushy grower; best grown in shade.

Gerburg Emmerich 234
Single; T soft rose-red with darker veins and blush; S soft rose-red with green tips; C smoky vivid purple-pink; trailer.

Gerhard Mathieu 195
Semi-double/double; T rose-red with grooves; S on the upper side green becoming darker towards the tip, red veins at base, underside pale strawberry-red shading to green towards the tip; C blue-violet, fading to purple-violet, at base white-pink, fancy whitish to pink splashes; large flower; very free-flowering; self-branching; upright grower; suitable for growing as a standard; for filtered light.

Gerharda's Aubergine 373
Single; T glossy reddish-purple; S upper side glossy reddish-purple with darker veins, underside deep-purple with reddish-purple veins; C deep burgundy-red, underside deep mahogany-coloured, at base deep-purple, dark-purple edges with brown glow; medium-sized flower; self-branching; beautiful dark-red branches; semi-trailer; can be grown as a trailer and as a standard; for full sun.

Gert Jan Bekamp 423 ·
Single; T creamy-white with orange blush; S pale carmine-pink with green tips; C crimson to carmine-red; medium-sized flower; upright grower; suitable for full sun.

Gina 437
Double; T deep-pink; S bright rose-red, underneath slightly paler, green tips; C white, at base rose-red, rose-red veins and rose-red splashes on the underside of the petals; rather large flower; very free-flowering; self-branching; trailer; easy to grow.

Gleneagles 47
Single/semi-double; T ivory-white with greenish glow; S clear white with pink glow, red marking at base, red edge, underneath white with red blush, green tips; C lilac, at base white; medium-sized flower; self-branching; upright bushy grower.

Glitters 481
Single; T deep salmon-pink with orange tinge; S deep salmon-pink with orange-coloured tinge, shading to cream, ending in green tips, on the underside pale salmon-pink; C deep-orange, at the base paler, darker veins; medium-sized flower; free-flowering; self-branching; upright bushy grower; tolerates full sun.

Glockenspiel 270
Double; T glossy rose-red; S glossy rose-red, with cream tips; C purple-violet with darker edge, at base carmine-red, red veins with carmine-red splash along it; rather large flower; very free-flowering; trailer.

Glowing Embers 488
Single; T dark-pink with darker grooves; S carmine-pink with grooves, on the underside deeper carmine-pink, green tips; C dark orange-red fading to violet-red, at base salmon- to pale pink, salmon-pink to orange splashes; medium-sized flower; very floriferous; flowers sometimes twice a year; branches well; grows with lax branches; suitable for semi-trailer; likes a place sheltered from rain and wind

Glowing Lilac 61
Double; T white with pink blush; S white with pink tips; C lilac, pink splashes in the middle; large flower; trailer.

Golden Arrow 464
Single; T pale pink-orange with orange stripes; S bright orange, at base paler, pale-green tips; C deep-orange with darker veins; long, slender flower; free-flowering but late; trailer; triphylla-type; prone to botrytis.

Golden Jubilee 484
Double; T salmon-pink with darker stripes; S vermillion-red changing to salmon-pink with orange splashes, underneath orange, green tips; C dull wine-red, fading to dull violet, orange to vermillion-red splashes, at base salmon-pink, wine-red edges, faint orange-red veins; medium-sized flower; semi-trailer; suitable to be trained for a basket.

Golden la Campanella 191
Semi-double; T ivory-white; S ivory-white with green flush, on the underside ivory-white with purple flush; C red-purple fading to violet-red, at the base carmine-red, red veins; medium-sized flower; free-flowering; self-branching; lovely variegated foliage; trailer.

Golden Multa 363
Single; T red; S red; C blue-purple, at base pink, rose-red veins; rather small flower; free-flowering; branches well; beautiful yellow-green foliage; lax grower; suitable for growing as a trailer.

Goldsworth Beauty 328
Single; T glossy rose-red; S glossy rose-red, large cream tips with small green dots; C slightly darker rose-red, at base pale-violet; medium-sized flower; upright grower.

Gordon's China Rose 130
Single/semi-double; T greenish-white with green stripes; S white with pink blush, long green tips; C lavender-blue-pink, fading to lilac, at base pale pink, darker edges, pink veins; medium-sized flower; self-branching; lax bushy grower; suitable as a semi-trailer; likes filtered light.

Gracie 401
Double; T rose-red with greenish flush and stripes; S rose-red with yellow-green tips; C deep-purple, at base rose-red; large flower; lax upright grower; suitable to be grown as a trailer; flower with very long sepals.

Graf Spee 427
Single; T clear white with green tinge and green stripes; S clear white, pink tinge, on the underside white with pink blush, yellow-green tips; C deep rose-red, at the base soft-pink feathery splashes, darker edge, red veins; large flower; very free-flowering; self-branching; upright lax grower; suitable as semi-trailer.

Green 'n Gold 387
Single; T medium rose-red with darker stripes; S medium rose-red, small green tips; C deep-purple; medium-sized flower; free-flowering; lovely variegated foliage; upright grower; needs full sun for best foliage-colouring.

Grimbeerd 147
Single; T white; S white with yellow-green tips; C deep-purple, at base pink; medium-sized flower; free-flowering; trailer.

Grumpy 374
Single; T cerise-red with darker stripes; S on the upper side cerise-red, on the underside crimson, small green tips; C deep blue-purple fading to dark blue-violet, at base crimson-pink, crimson-pink veins; small flower held out; very floriferous; self branching; upright grower; requires filtered light.

Gruss an Graz 131
Single; T white with green blush and green stripes; S white with pink blush, towards the tips shading to yellow-green, at base red edges, on the underside candy-pink, green tips; C violet, at the base pink, red veins; medium-sized flower; free-flowering; self-branching; lax upright grower; suitable for growing as a trailer; needs a shaded site.

Guurtje 306
Double; T greenish-white with pink tinge and pink veins; S upper side white with pink blush, underside rose-red, green tips; C violet, at base pink and many pink splashes; large flower; free-flowering; self-branching; semi-trailer; can be grown as a trailer or bush; dislikes full sun.

Gwen Dodge 45
Single; T palest waxy-pink; S pale-pink; C violet, at base white; medium-sized flower held out; very floriferous; self-branching; upright grower; can be grown as a standard or a table-standard.

Hanau 138
Single; T white with green blush, at base crimson; S glossy white, at base crimson-purple, underside white, at base a touch of pink, pale-green tips; C deep-purple, at base white, red veins with pale-pink splash; large flower; self-branching; upright grower; for semi-shade.

Hanna 443
Double; T glossy carmine-red; S glossy carmine-red, green tips; C clear white, at base red and from base red veins; medium-sized flower; very floriferous; upright grower; strong plant.

Hans Peter Peters 181
Single; T carmine-pink with darker stripes; S white with pink blush, underside carmine-pink, green tips; C vivid-pink, at the base carmine-pink, darker veins; medium-sized flower; self-branching; upright grower; suitable for growing as a standard.

Hans van de Beek 124
Single; T pale yellow-green; S upper side pink, underside phlox-pink, large green tips; C blue-violet; semi-trailer; needs position in filtered light.

Haus Wiesengrund 301
Single; T strawberry-red with red stripes; S crimson shading to cyclamen-red, carmine-red veins, underside cyclamen-pink with carmine-red streak, green tips; C dull purple, at the base pale pink, red veins; medium-sized flower; very floriferous; self-branching; upright grower; for full sun; suitable for training as a standard.

Hazel 109
Double; T rose-red; S rose-red with green tips; C lavender-blue fading to pale violet, pale-pink at base, many petaloids; large flower; flowers freely and over a long period; trailer; requires a shady site.

Hellas 29
Semi-double; T pale-pink; S pink, underside darker pink; C white with palest pink veins; medium-sized flower; self-branching; lax upright grower; can be grown as a semi-trailer; needs filtered light.

Hendrik den Besten 361
Semi-double; T rose-red; S rose-red with absinth-green tips; C dark robin-red; semi-trailer; needs a position in filtered light.

Hendrina Bovenschen 126
Single; T white with green blush and stripes; S upper side white with carmine-pink blush, underside candy-pink; C purple-violet fading to cyclamen-pink, at base pale-pink; rather large flower; free-flowering; needs careful pinching; upright stiff grower.

Hendrina Josephina 353
Single; T light rose-red; S light rose-red shading to pale yellow-green tips, underneath light red; C red; small flower; free-flowering; self-branching; trailer; heat-tolerant.

Hercules 303
Single; T vivid rose-red; S rose-red with lighter splashes; C violet; medium-sizer flower; upright grower.

Herjan de Groot 27
Single; T palest purple-pink with yellow-green tinge; S pale purple-pink with darker veins; C white with red-purple tinge; medium-sized flower; self-branching; lax upright grower; requires a place in shade.

Herman de Graaff 433
Single; T aubergine-red, darker stripes; S vivid rose-red, small olive-green tips; C white, at the base vivid rose-red, from base vivid rose-red veins; medium-sized flower; free-flowering; trailer.

Hermie Kainz 407
Single; T white with pink blush; S white with pink blush; C rose-red, at base lighter; medium-sized flower; free-flowering; trailer.

Herzilein 327
Single; T soft-red; S paler soft-red, underside scarlet-red, green tips; C scarlet-red with a tinge orange; small flower held out; very floriferous; self-branching; upright grower; for full sun; lovely fuchsia.

Heston Blue 84
Semi-double; T white, green at base; S white with pink blush, underside carmine-pink, towards the tips shading to white, green tips; C lilac-blue fading to mauve, at base white, darker edges; rather large flower; needs careful pinching; bushy grower; needs a cool position in shade.

Hilda 284
Semi-double; T rose-red; S rose-red shading to white, green tips; C lilac, at base pink, darker edges, carmine stripes from base; rather large flower; free-flowering; upright grower.

Hilchenbacher Grusz 110
Double; T white with green blush; S clear white with green tips; C lilac, at base white; rather large flower; free-flowering; self-branching; trailer.

Hölderlin 222
Single; T soft-pink and white splashed; S soft pink with darker veins, underside carmine-red; C vivid red-purple, at base vermillion-red; rather small flower; free-flowering; self-branching; upright grower; can be grown as a pyramid; tolerates full sun.

Huize Ruurlo 334
Single; T carmine-pink; S carmine-red, with light tip on the underside, small green dots; C dull crimson, at base lighter; medium-sized flower; free-flowering; upright grower; can be grown as a standard and as a semi-trailer; suitable for a place in full sun.

Humboldt Holiday 218
Double; T white with pink blush; S splashy white with pink blush, green tips; C violet fading to red-violet, at the base white, dark-violet edges, carmine-pink veins, many pink splashes; large flower; trailer; needs a sheltered and shaded condition.

Humiko Kamo 143
Double; T white with green blush; S white with pink blush, underside pink-purple; C pale blue-violet, at base paler to white, dark blue-violet edges; rather large flower; self-branching; semi-trailer; for filtered light.

I

Ice Maiden 17
Double; T ivory-white with green tinge; S ivory-white with pink edges, underside ivory-white with pink at base, long green tips; C white with a green tinge; large full flower; free-flowering; self-branching; needs careful pinching; trailer; requires a sheltered place.

Igloo Maid 10
Double; T white with green tinge and green stripes; S white; underside white with pink tinge; C white, in the sun fading to white with pink tinge, at the base pale pink; medium-sized flower; self-branching; yellow-green foliage; upright bushy grower; for shade.

Imperial Fantasy 171
Double; T greenish-white with green grooves; S white with green tinge, underside clear white, yellow-green tips; C blue-purple, at base white, white veins and a faint lilac splash through the centre; medium-sized flower; free-flowering; needs regular and careful pinching; trailer; for filtered light.

Ingelore 247
Single; T carmine-red; S carmine-red; C violet, at the base pink, darker edges; medium-sized flower; upright grower; dwarf; slow-growing; for full sun.

Insulinde 465
Single; T pale tomato-red; S pale tomato-red, darker edges and darker tips; C tomato-red; long, slender flower; free-flowering; self-branching; upright grower; needs filtered light; triphylla-type.

Isle of Mull 302
Single; T purple-pink with darker stripes; S pale-pink with pale-red veins, green tips; C pink-purple fading to pink, at base paler, darker edges, vivid-pink splashes; medium-sized flower; very floriferous, early-flowering; branches well; bushy grower with short joints; likes a somewhat sheltered site in semi-shade.

Italiano 399
Double; T salmon-pink with darker grooves; S deep rose-red with darker grooves, on the underside carmine-pink, green tips; C deep-purple fading to violet; at base carmine-red, faint red veins, orange splashes; medium-sized flower; free-flowering; self-branching; trailer; needs a sheltered place in shade.

J

Jaap Brummel 424
Semi-double/double; T pale yellow-green becoming paler towards the tips; S upper side cream with green tinge, with pale red-purple blush at the base, underside pale red-purple, bright green tip; C deep robin-red, base pink; medium-sized flower; free-flowering; upright vigorous grower; for filtered light.

Jacqueline 317
Single; T scarlet-red; S scarlet-red, underside geranium-pink; C vermillion-red, at the base orange, reddish veins and orange splash; long slender flower; very floriferous; upright grower; suitable for full sun; triphylla-type.

Jacques Crasborn 495
Semi-double; T palest rose-red; S palest crimson; C pale pink-orange; medium-sized flower; very floriferous; self-branching; trailer; for filtered light.

Jan van Maasakkers 194
Single; T pale pink-purple with darker grooves; S pale pink-purple, underneath pink-purple, green tips; C pale fuchsia-purple, at base palest pink-purple; medium-sized flower; trailer; for filtered light; flowers do not fade.

Jan zonder Vrees 186
Semi-double; T glossy green with pink tinge; S upper side white with green tinge and green veins, underside white with pink blush, green tips; C bright violet-purple, fading to purple-violet, at the base deep carmine-pink, darker edges, from base red veins; small flower; very floriferous; self-branching; upright grower; for filtered light.

Jandel 112
Semi-double/double; T white with green grooves; S white with carmine-pink edges and splashes, underside white with carmine-pink tinge, green tips; C lavender-purple, fading to pale purple-violet, at base white; medium-sized flower; free-flowering; upright grower with stiff horizontal branches; suitable for full sun and shade; can be grown as a standard.

Jane Humber 213
Double; T waxy-white with green and red stripes; S on the upper side white with a touch of pink, on the underside appleblossom-pink, green tips; C lilac, maturing to amethyst-violet, at base pale pink, red veins; medium-sized flower; free-flowering; self-branching; trailer; requires filtered light.

Janna 316
Single; T light rose-red with rose-red stripes; S light rose-red, on the underside fading (from the base) from light rose-red to white, large green tips; C cerise-red, at base dull scarlet-red; long slender flower; free-flowering; upright grower; suitable for full sun.

Janna Roddenhof 382
Semi-double; T carmine-pink; S carmine-pink; C deep beetroot-red, at base carmine-pink; large flower; free-flowering; self-branching; tall upright grower.

Janneke Brinkman-Salentijn 377
Single; T deep glossy red-purple; S dark red-purple, underside red-purple; C dark red-purple; smallish flower; rather free-flowering; self-branching; compact upright grower; requires a shady site.

Japmar Hofmeyer 354
Single; T light-red; S red, on the underside slightly lighter red; C purple-red, pink edges and red veins; small flower; free-flowering; lax upright grower; can be grown as a semi-trailer.

Jaspers Duimelot 176
Single; T shell-pink with green tinge; S shell-pink, underside bright pink, green tips; C bright fuchsia-purple, at base soft shell-pink; medium-sized flower; self-branching; trailer; tolerates sun.

Jaspers Groentje 149
Single; T white with green tinge; S waxy white with green tinge, bright green tips; C bright cyclamen-red, at the base pink-purple veins and mauve splash; medium-sized flower held out; very floriferous; self-branching; upright grower; resistant to full sun; best colours however in filtered light; a rather unruly grower needing regular and careful pruning.

Jaspers Ringeling 294
Semi-double; T rose-red; S rose-red, underside candy-pink, small green tips; C dull lilac-purple, at base very soft pink; medium-sized flower; free-flowering; needs careful pinching; semi-trailer; requires condition in filtered light.

Jaspers Vuurbal 345
Double; T rose-red; S rose-red with green tips; C red-purple with paler splashes; medium-sized flower; free-flowering; branches well; lax grower; suitable as semi-trailer.

Jaspers Wentelwiek 244
Single; T light carmine-pink with slightly darker stripes; S spotted carmine-red, at base and edges carmine-red, underside appleblossom-pink, green tips; C purple-blue, at base lighter; medium-sized flower with long curved tube; self-branching; trailer; suitable for full sun.

Javelin 315
Single; T crimson; S on the upper side cardinal-red, on the underside crimson; C deep red; medium-sized flower; very free- and early flowering; upright grower; for full sun; suitable for growing as a standard or pillar.

Jean 478
Single; T whitish-pink with green tinge; S coral-pink, on the underside vermillion-red, green tips; C vermillion-red, underside orange, at the base pale-orange and orange splashes; medium-sized flower; free-flowering; trailer; tolerates full sun; suitable to be grown for baskets and as an espalier.

Jeanette Schwab 311
Single; T rose-red; S rose-red, on the underside pale rose-red, large yellow-green tips; C bright carmine-red; long slender flower; free-flowering; self-branching; do not pinch too much! Primary crossing.

Jeeves 287
Semi-double; T deep-red; S scarlet-red, on the underside cerise-red, small green tips; C violet maturing to purple, at base cerise-red, darker edges, red veins with reddish-orange splash along it; medium-sized flower; upright grower.

Jess 409
Single; T white with pink blush; S deep pink to the tips fading to paler pink, finishing in yellow-green tips; C bright cerise-red, at the base pale-pink; medium-sized flower; free-flowering; trailer.

Joan Gilbert 267
Double; T glossy rose-red; S waxy-rose-red with darker grooves, on the underside carmine-red, green tips; C purple-blue, maturing to violet, many carmine-pink and salmon-coloured splashes, at base lilac, darker edges and carmine-red veins, the petaloids are carmine-pink with violet splashes; medium-sized flower; branches well; upright bushy grower; requires shade.

Joan Leach 293
Single; T bright rose-red; S bright rose-red; C pale lavender-blue, at base paler, pink blush; medium-sized flower; very floriferous; branches well; upright bushy grower with spreading branches; dwarf.

Joan's Delight 378
Single; T carmine-red; S carmine-red; C deep violet-blue; small flower; free-flowering; self-branching; upright grower; dwarf; suitable for small pots; best colour in shade.

Joanne 65
Double; T rose-red; S rose-red; C pink-lilac, at base carmine-red veins; large lower; upright grower; can be grown as a semi-trailer.

Joe Kushber 174
Double; T waxy-white with green tinge; S waxy-white, underside white with pink blush, pink tips; C deep violet-blue maturing to lilac-purple, at base pink, dark lilac edges, red and dark-blue veins, many blue petaloids; large full flower; reasonable flowering; self-branching; upright, bushy, somewhat lax grower; suitable to be trained as a standard; needs shade.

Joker 341
Semi-double; T rose-red; S rose-red lighter towards the tips, green tips; C multicoloured red, red veins and blue-purple tinge; rather large flower; very free-flowering; self-branching; trailer; needs a cool sheltered place in shade; this fuchsia does not flower abundantly before the second year.

Joop van Brakel 266
Double; T creamy-pink with darker grooves; S on the upper side creamy-pink fading to a green tip, on the underside pale rose-red; C rose-red with blue tinge, at base lighter, the outer petals with pale-purple edges and pink-orange splashes; rather large loose flower; trailer; requires filtered light.

Joyce Sinton 243
Single; T glossy baby-pink with strawberry-red stripes; S pale rose-red, underside geranium-pink, green tips; C blood-red, at the base geranium-pink, darker edges and faint veins with orange splash along it; rather large flower held out somewhat; free-flowering; self-branching; upright grower; suitable for full sun; can be grown as a standard.

Julia 258
Double; T glossy crimson; S glossy crimson, green tips; C mauve-purple, at the base carmine-red, red veins; large flower; reasonable flowering; self-branching; trailer; sun-tolerant.

Jülchen 411
Single; T waxy-white with green tinge; S waxy-white changing to pink, on the underside pink; C dull strawberry-red, white at the base, faint white veins; smallish flower; very floriferous; self-branching; upright grower; for full sun; can be grown as a pyramid.

Julicka 350
Single; T strawberry-red with darker stripes; S crimson with white streak over the centre, on the underside crimson; C blue-purple, maturing to purple, at base carmine-pink, violet-blue edge, red veins; rather large flower; very free-flowering; self-branching; tall upright grower; requires filtered light.

Jupiter Seventy 479
Single; T cream with pink blush; S cream with a touch of scarlet, underside ancient-pink, pale green tips; C light scarlet, at the base orange, darker veins and orange splash; medium-sized flower; free-flowering; self-branching; upright grower; for full sun; heat-resistant.

K

Karina 368
Single; T bright carmine-red; S bright carmine-red, lighter towards the tip; C purple-lilac, fading to pale purple, at the base pink, rose-red veins; rather small flower; flowers freely and over a long period; self-branching; upright grower; strong plant.

Kathy Louise 289
Double; T carmine-red; S glossy carmine-red, on the underside slightly lighter; C light lavender-blue, at base slightly darker, rose-red veins; large flower; free-flowering; trailer; needs a lot of pinching early in the season; best in shade.

Kathy's Sparkler 272
Double; T glossy pale rose-red; S deep-pink, on the underside carmine-pink, green tips; C deep-lavender-blue, maturing to mauve, at the base pale mauve, red veins, irregular white and pink splashes; medium-sized flower; self-branching; lax upright grower; likes a sheltered position; suitable for baskets and standards.

Kati 441
Double; T light rose-red; S creamy-pink to pale rose-red, large green tips; C white with pink veins; medium-sized flower; upright grower.

Katie 170
Single; T waxy ivory-white with pink blush; S waxy ivory-white with pink blush, green tips; C lilac-pink, at base pale pink, darker streak and pale-pink splash; medium-sized flower; very floriferous; self-branching; lax upright grower; suitable for growing as a trailer.

Katinka 474
Single; T Bengal-pink; S Bengal-pink, underside light lac-red; C rose-red, at base pink, darker edges; small flower held out; flowers freely and over a long period; upright grower; for full sun; primary crossing.

Kay Riley 39
Double; T pink; S pink; C pink with white splashes; large flower; trailer.

Ken Goldsmith 476
Single; T pink-orange; S pink-orange, lighter towards the small pale-green tips; C clear orange; medium-sized flower with long tube; upright grower; triphylla-type.

Ken Jennings 95
Single; T white with touch of pink; S pink, on the underside pale-pink; C violet, maturing to dark pink-violet, at the base pink, faint pale-pink veins; medium-sized flower; upright bushy grower; suitable for growing as a standard.

Kentish Maid 206
Single; T flesh-coloured with darker stripes; S marbled pale- to carmine-pink, underside pale carmine-pink, green tips; C deep mauve, shading to pale violet, at base cream, pink veins; medium-sized flower; very floriferous; self-branching; upright grower; for semi-shade; can be grown as a standard.

Kerry Ann 162
Single; T pale pink with green grooves; S deep pink with darker grooves, on the underside darker pink, green tips; C deep violet-blue, fading to pale purple, at base paler and white splash, deep-pink veins; medium-sized flower; free-flowering; self-branching; upright bushy grower with short joints; likes a sheltered site; a strong fuchsia.

Keystone 21
Single; T glossy light cerise-red with darker stripes; S pale pink, from base a carmine edge, green tips; C pale pink, at base pink, faint pink veins; medium-sized flower; self-branching; upright bushy grower; tolerates full sun; prone to botrytis.

Kim Broekhof 483
Single; T deep orange-pink with greenish stripes; S flamingo-pink, towards the base shading to orange-pink, on the underside deep coral-pink, absinth-green tips; C pale tomato-red, at base pale orange-pink, orange splashes; small, long flower; free-flowering; self-branching; upright grower or semi-trailer; can be grown as a trailer and as a bush; the best colour is achieved if kept in filtered light.

Kit Oxtoby 63
Double; T porcelain-white; S pale pink with green tips; C pale lilac, shading to candy-pink towards the edges, pale-pink splashes along the faint red veins; medium-sized flower; free-flowering; semi-trailer; for full sun.

Knights Errant 88
Single; T clear white; S clear white with green tips; C lilac, white at the base; medium-sized flower; lax upright grower.

Königin der Frühe 385
Single; T glossy deep red with darker stripes; S upper side glossy dark red, underside crimson, small green tips; C bright violet-purple, fading to purple-violet, at base crimson, red veins and crimson splash; rather small flower; very floriferous; upright grower; sun-tolerant; can be grown as a standard.

Koning Nobel 163
Single; T ivory-white; S ivory-white with green tips; C blue-violet; medium-sized flower; trailer.

Kyoto 431
Single; T red; S red to pale aubergine-coloured; C white with purple-red veins; medium-sized flower; free-flowering; self-branching; upright grower with horizontal branches; resistant to full sun; lovely-shaped flower.

L

La Courneuve Fleury 319
Single; T red to aubergine-coloured; S pale aubergine-coloured with ivory-white tips; C aubergine-coloured to beetroot-red; long slender flower; free-flowering; lax upright grower.

La Fiesta 175
Double; T white with green tinge and green stripes; S white with green stripes, underside white, green tips; C purple-violet, maturing to lilac-purple, at the base white, red veins, from base spiraea-red splash; rather large flower; self-branching; trailer with stiff branches; needs filtered light; not an easy one.

Lavaglut 330
Single; T red; S glossy red with darker stripes; C red-purple, at base bright red, red veins; medium-sized flower with wide-spreading corolla; very floriferous; self-branching; upright grower; requires filtered light; can be grown as a standard or pyramid.

Lavender Kate 216
Double; T pink; S pink, on the underside deeper pink; C lavender-blue with darker splashes; rather large flower; upright grower.

Lechlade Gorgon 199
Single; T pale violet-purple; S pale violet-purple, on the underside petunia-purple; C lilac-mauve; small flower held out; late flowering; upright grower; for full sun; can well be grown as a standard; primary crossing.

Lee Antony 79
Single; T very soft pink, at base pink; S very soft pink, underside darker pink; C candy-pink; long slender flower; free-flowering; upright grower; triphylla-type.

Leine Perle 432
Single; T carmine-red; S carmine-red with green tips; C white, carmine-red veins from base; medium-sized bell-shaped flower; very free-flowering; self-branching; upright grower; suitable for full sun.

Len Bielby 227
Single; T scarlet-red; S on the upper side currant-red, on the underside azalea-pink; C mandarin-red; long slender flower; very floriferous; resistant to full sun; triphylla-type.

Leodien 310
Single; T pale yellow-green with pink blush; S pink; C dull fuchsia-purple, at base flesh-pink; medium-sized flower; self-branching; likes filtered light.

Les Hobbs 339
Single; T deep carmine-pink with darker stripes; S strawberry-red, on the underside somewhat brighter coloured, small white tips; C bright red, velvet tinge; medium-sized flower; free-flowering; upright flower; suitable for full sun.

Lican Ray 51
Single; T white with green stripes; S on the upper side white with a touch of pink, green streak through the centre, on the underside cherry-pink, green tips; C lilac, fading to violet, at base pink, darker edges, red veins and pink splash; medium-sized flower; self-branching; upright grower; for filtered light.

Lichtendorf 362
Single/semi-double; T glossy rose-red with currant-red stripes; S crimson, small green tips; C bright violet-purple, at base crimson, dark violet-purple edges, red veins with crimson splash; medium-sized flower; free-flowering; self-branching; upright grower; for filtered light; a strong fuchsia.

Lidi 135
Double; T white with green tinge; S white, green at base, and green tips; C deep purple; medium-sized flower.

Lidie Bartelink 343
Single; T crimson; S carmine-red changing to carmine-pink, on the underside bright carmine-red, yellow-green tips; C robin-red, at base carmine-red, darker edges, red veins; small flower; very free-flowering; self-branching; trailer; for full sun.

Liebelei 435
Single; T crimson-pink; S crimson-pink with green tips; C white, crimson veins; medium-sized flower; upright grower.

Liesbeth Jansen 381
Double; T deep carmine-pink; S carmine-pink, underside crimson, green tips; C deep-violet, at base crimson, darker edges and crimson veins; medium-sized flower; a hardy fuchsia.

Lilac Dainty 392
Double; T dull-red; S dull-red, on the underside carmine-red; C lilac, at the base red, darker edges, pink veins and red splash; smallish flower; free-flowering; upright bushy grower.

Lilo Vogt 225
Single; T rose-red; S pale pink, underside pink, green tips; C rose-red; long slender flower; free-flowering; trailer; likes a sheltered site.

Linda Copley 23
Double; T pink; S pink, green tips; C pink, at base carmine-red, from base carmine-red veins; large flower; free-flowering over a long period; trailer.

Linda Goulding 28
Single; T waxy-white with green tinge and stripes; S white with pink blush, pink edges, on the underside splashy pink, green tips; C white, pale-pink veins; medium-sized, bell-shaped flower; very floriferous; branches well; upright grower; suitable for growing as a standard or pillar.

Lindisfarne 85
Single/semi-double; T greenish-white with pink tinge; S palest pink, green tips; C deep blue-purple, maturing to violet-purple, at the base pink, pink veins; medium-sized; very floriferous; branches well with short joints; upright bushy grower; suitable for growing as a table-standard.

Lindsay Hendrickx 155
Single; T white with a greenish touch; S white with a greenish touch and green tips; C deep purple-blue, at the base pink; long slender flower; free-flowering; trailer.

Little John 197
Single; T crimson-purple; S spiraea-pink, on the underside magenta-pink, olive-green tips; C deep purple-violet, at base white, purple veins and white splash; small flower; free-flowering; self-branching; trailer; for filtered light.

Loch Lomond 298
Single; T crimson with darker stripes; S from base shading from carmine-red to carmine-pink, underside crimson, large green tips; C petunia-purple, at base carmine-pink, beetroot-red edges, dark-red veins with carmine-pink splash; free-flowering; trailer; resistant to full sun; flower grows sideways on the flower-stalk.

Long Distance 223
Single; T pale fuchsia-red; S carmine-red; C carmine-pink; long slender flower; self-branching; for filtered light.

Long John 299
Single; T pale purple-pink with cyclamen-purple stripes; S on the upper side fuchsia-purple with darker stripes, on the underside pale purple-pink, pale brown-green tips; C fuchsia-purple, at base mauve-purple; long slender flower; free-flowering; trailer with graceful curved branches; requires a sheltered site in semi-shade; not an easy fuchsia!

Lorna Swinbank 46
Single; T white with pink blush; S white with pink blush, underside pale pink, green tips; C soft-blue, maturing to soft lilac-blue, at base white; upright grower; likes a shaded position.

Lotterer Queen 367
Semi-double/double; T crimson with white stripes; S on the upper side crimson, on the underside red, small white tips, the sepals are at base grown together; C bright violet-purple, at base rose-red, darker edge, red veins and rose-red splash; rather large flower; very free-flowering; self-branching; upright grower; needs a place in filtered light; suitable to be trained as a standard or pillar.

Lottie Hobby 355
Single; T scarlet-red; S red with paler tips; C scarlet-red; small flower; free- and early-flowering; self-branching; upright bushy grower; a hardy fuchsia.

Lubbertje Hop 164
Single; T ivory-white with pale-green tinge and green stripes; S on the upper side ivory-white with pale-green tinge and pink blush, on the underside ivory-white with pink blush, darker edges, large yellow-green tips; C dark blue-purple, maturing to cyclamen-purple, at base a touch white, red veins; medium-sized flower; upright grower; for filtered light and semi-shade; suitable for growing as a pillar.

Luscious 346
Double; T cerise-red; S cerise-red with yellow-green tips; C dull wine-red, shading towards the base to cerise-red, orange and pink, at base pale orange-red, orange-red veins, pink and orange splashes; large flower; lax upright grower; can be grown as a trailer; requires a sheltered place; needs careful pinching in spring; difficult to grow.

Lutgerdina 75
Single; T white with green tinge; S white with pink blush at base, pink edges, on the underside shading from cherry-pink at base to cyclamen-red on the tips, small green splashes; C soft lilac fading to soft violet, bright lilac edges and red veins; small flower; free-flowering; self-branching; upright grower; for filtered light; suitable for growing as a standard.

M

Mabejo 133
Double; T ivory-white with green glow, a touch of purple, green stripes; S white with green glow, red edges, on the underside white with carmine-red blush, green tips; C blue-violet fading to purple-violet, at the base pink, darker edges, red veins, many petaloids, blue-violet; medium-sized flower; self-branching; trailer; needs careful pruning to get a good shape.

Madame Cornelissen 436
Single; T bright carmine-red; S bright carmine-red; C white, at base carmine-red, red veins; rather small flower; free-flowering; upright grower; for full sun; suitable for growing as a standard; hardy.

Magic Flute 490
Single; T waxy-white with pink tinge; S waxy-white with pink tinge, green tips; C coral-red, at base white; medium-sized flower; early and reasonable flowering; trailer; suitable for containers.

Magilda 376
Single; T crimson with stripes; S crimson, on the underside vivid rose-red, small green tips; C violet-blue, fading to purple, at base pale rose-red, darker edges, red veins; medium-sized flower; free-flowering; upright grower; for filtered light.

Mallemolen 274
Single; T greenish-white with green stripes; S on the upper side pale rose-red, shading to pale-purple, green tips, on the underside pink; C dark and bright violet-purple; medium-sized flower; semi-trailer; for filtered light.

Mama Bleuss 280
Double; T rose-red with darker stripes; S pink, at the base dark rose-red; C lilac-blue, at the base pink, rose-red veins; large flower; free-flowering; branches well; lax upright grower; can be grown as a semi-trailer or as a 'weeping' standard; for filtered light.

Maresi 90
Single; T white with green blush; S white with pink blush, underside pink; C purple-blue; medium-sized flower; very floriferous; trailer; suitable for baskets.

Margaret Rose 296
Single; T white with pink blush; S upper side pale pink, underside pale purple-pink, pale streak over the centre, green tips; C magnolia-purple with darker edges, at base white, pale-red veins; medium-sized flower; upright bushy grower; for semi-shade.

Marloesje ter Beek 338
Double; T vivid rose-red; S vivid rose-red becoming lighter towards the tips, small green tips; C dull rose-red, at base faint pale splash; medium-sized flower; trailer.

Martien van Vugt 318
Single; T bright red; S bright red with darker small tips; C spiraea-red, at the base tomato-red, faint red veins; long slender flower; early and very free-flowering; self-branching; trailer; for full sun; needs a lot of pinching.

Martin's Catharina 471
Single; T pale yellow-green with pale-purple blush; S light red-purple, shading to pale yellow-green tips, underside light red-purple; C dark red-purple; small flower held out; free-flowering; self-branching; upright grower; for filtered light.

Martin's Leencor 375
Semi-double; T vivid rose-red; S vivid rose-red; C deep-purple, at the base rose-red; medium-sized flower; upright grower.

Martin's Yellow Surprise 458
Single; T green-yellow with soft-pink blush; S green-yellow, underside paler; C pale green-yellow; long slender flower; upright grower; primary crossing.

Marty 283
Double; T pink with green blush and darker stripes; S pink with darker stripes; C violet, paler splashes at base; large flower; reasonable flowering; lax upright grower or semi-trailer.

Marylin Olsen 430
Single; T rose-red; S rose-red, green tips; C white, at base rose-red; medium-sized flower; free-flowering; branches well; upright grower.

Max Jaffa 165
Single; T pink with pale-purple blush; S phlox-pink, on the underside pale fuchsia-purple, bright green tips; C bright fuchsia-purple, at the base carmine-pink, light-red veins and pale-pink splash; medium-sized flower; very floriferous; branches reasonable; upright grower; for filtered light; needs careful pinching.

Medalist 71
Double; T bright pink with darker stripes; S bright pink, underside slightly darker; C white with pink blush and many pink petaloïds; large flushy flower; lax upright grower or stiff trailer; requires cool conditions.

Medusa 452
Single; T crimson; S crimson; C white, at base crimson, crimson veins; large flower; trailer; for filtered light.

Merimbula Giant 279
Double; T dark crimson; S dark crimson with small pale tips; C white with a touch of pink, at base very dark crimson, rose-red veins with rose-red splashes; rather large flower; reasonable flowering; trailer; for a shaded place.

Mia Goedman 43
Single; T light coral-pink; S on the upper side coral-pink, underside soft-pink, pale green tips; C purple-mauve, at the base pink; long slender flower; free-flowering; upright grower; sun-tolerant.

Michel Schwab 462
Single; T soft-red; S red-orange, underside orange, orange-yellow tips; C bright red; long slender flower; needs a lot of light; primary crossing.

Mieke Alferink 480
Single; T deep rose-red; S light tomato-red, on the underside dull orange, small green tips; C vermillion-red, at the base orange-red, orange-red veins and orange-red splash; medium-sized flower; free-flowering; upright grower; suitable for full sun; can be grown as a pillar.

Mieke Meursing 292
Single; T glossy cerise-red; S glossy cerise-red; C mauve, at base cerise-red, cerise-red veins; medium-sized flower; free-flowering; self-branching; bushy upright grower; for a sheltered site; can be grown as a standard.

Mina Knudde 148
Single; T pale pink with pink blush and candy-pink veins; S pale pink with pink blush and candy-pink veins, on the underside candy-pink, large green tips; C violet-purple, fading to beetroot-red, at base pale pink, reddish edges, candy-pink veins and pale pink splash; rather large flower; free-flowering; self-branching; trailer; for filtered light.

Mini 91
Single; T white with pink tinge and pink stripes; S white with pink blush and green tips; C deep-violet; small flower held out; free-flowering; self-branching; upright grower; dwarfish-growing bush; there is another cultivar named 'Mini', whose sepals are strawberry-red.

Misty Blue 49
Double; T pale pink; S pale pink, on the underside soft crimson-pink, green tips; C lilac-blue, at base pale pink, soft crimson-pink veins; medium-sized very full flower; free-flowering; upright bushy grower.

Misty Haze 53
Double; T greenish-white with green stripes; S white with green tips; C pale lavender-blue, at the base white, red veins, pink splashes, many petaloids; large flower; bushy upright grower; requires a shaded and sheltered place; graceful fuchsia; can be grown as trailer or standard.

Mollie Beaulah 78
Double; T ivory-white with green tinge; S light cyclamen-red with darker edges, on the underside light-red, green tips; C Bengal-red, at base pale pink, soft-red edges, faint red veins and light-red splash; medium-sized flower; free-flowering; semi-trailer; needs a sheltered position, best grown in greenhouse or covered terrace.

Mon Amie 62
Double; T green-white with pink blush and green stripes; S marbled pink, shading to greenish-white, on the underside candy-pink, white tips with small green dot; C phlox-pink with darker edges and red veins; rather large flower; free-flowering; upright grower; for full sun.

Montalba 7
Single/semi-double; T white with obvious red stripes, at base red; S on the upper side white with greenish tinge and stripes, at base somewhat red, on the underside white, at base a touch red, red edges and green tips; C white with faint pink veins; medium-sized flower; very free-flowering; self-branching; upright grower with strong red branches; can be grown in many shapes.

Monte Negro 309
Single; T magenta-pink with darker stripes; S on the upper side robin-red, on the underside magenta-pink, pale green tips; C dark robin-red with darker veins; medium-sized flower; free- and early- flowering; self-branching; upright grower; can be grown as a semi-trailer; needs filtered light.

Monte Rosa 24
Double; T pink with green and red stripes; S pink-white with green tips; C white, at the base pink, pink veins; large flower; free-flowering over a long period, but late in flower; upright grower; needs support.

Montevideo 69
Double; T flesh-pink; S flesh-pink with pale-green tips; C lilac-pink, at base flesh-pink; medium-sized flower; free-flowering; trailer.

Monty Python 461
Single; T pale carmine-pink with darker stripes; S pink, on the underside light tomato-red, at base vermillion-red, pale-green tips; C bright orange with red veins; long slender flower; trailer; requires filtered light; triphylla-type.

More Applause 55
Double; T white with green stripes; S upper side ivory-white with soft pink blush, underside pink, pale-green tips; C lavender-pink, at base white, red veins, large petaloids; large flower; late-flowering; self-branching; trailer; for filtered light.

Mötti 20
Single; T ivory-white with green tinge and green stripes; S upper side pale-mauve with darker rose-red edges, changing to ivory-white, underside cyclamen-pink, small yellow-green tips; C pale shell-pink with cyclamen-pink veins; small flower; very floriferous; semi-trailer; for full sun.

Mrs Susan Brookfield 203
Double; T glossy white with rose-red blush; S vivid, dark rose-red; C rose-purple, at base lighter; medium-sized flower; upright grower.

Mrs Marshall 412
Single; T waxy-white; S waxy-white with pink tinge, underside pale pink, green tips; C rose-red, at base white, slightly darker edges; medium-sized flower; free-flowering; self-branching; upright bushy grower; needs a cool place in shade; suitable to be trained in many shapes.

My Dear 104
Double; T waxy-white with green stripes; S greenish-white, short red veins from base, green tips; C bright lavender-blue, maturing to lavender-pink, at base white, rose-red veins and faint pink splash; rather small flower; early- and free-flowering; upright grower; for filtered light.

New Fascination 454
Double; T carmine-red; S carmine-red, underside carmine-red with orange tinge; C soft-pink with lilac blush, at the base carmine-red, lilac-pink edges and obvious red veins; rather large flower; upright grower; for full sun; needs careful pinching; suitable for growing as a standard.

Nici's Findling 246
Single; T ivory-white with a touch of pink and darker grooves; S glossy carmine-pink with darker blush, on the underside pale tomato-red, yellow-green tips; C pale cardinal-red, on the underside more orange, pale tomato-red splash from the base; rather small flower; very floriferous; self-branching; upright grower; for full sun; can be grown as a bush or as a pyramid.

Nicky Veerman 18
Single; T porcelain-white with green stripes; S on the upper side porcelain-white, on the underside white, small green tips; C pink, pale purple-pink edge and veins; rather small flower; very floriferous; self-branching; upright grower with stiff branches; for full sun; can be grown as a standard or pyramid.

Nuwenspete 348
Single; T glossy red; S glossy red; C violet, fading to purple-violet, at the base pink, red veins and pale-pink splashes; medium-sized flower held out; early- and free-flowering; upright grower; for filtered light.

O

Obergärtner Koch 468
Single; T bright orange; S bright orange; C bright orange; long slender flower; free-flowering; upright grower; triphylla-type.

Olympic Lass 54
Double; T white; S white; C lavender-pink; large flower; reasonable flowering; trailer.

Orangeblossom 494
Single; T soft peach-pink with darker grooves; S soft peach-pink, small green tips; C bright orange; small flower; free-flowering; lax upright grower; suitable for containers and small baskets.

Orange Glow 487
Single; T light reddish; S light carmine-red, on the underside orange; C smoky orange, at the base vivid-orange, red veins; medium-sized flower held out; branches with difficulty; for full sun; can be grown as a standard; needs a lot of pinching.

Oriental Sunrise 473
Single; T glossy soft-pink; S pale pinkish-red, on the underside orange-pink; green tips; C vermillion-red, at the base orange; medium-sized flower; free-flowering; self-branching; lax upright grower or semi-trailer; for full sun.

Ostfriesland 150
Single; T ivory-white with pink flush and faint green stripes; S white with pink blush, green tips; C magenta, at the base white, red veins with carmine-pink splash; medium-sized flower; free-flowering; self-branching; semi-trailer; for filtered light.

P

Pabbe's Blikoortje 160
Single/semi-double; T glossy white with pink blush and green stripes; S glossy white with a touch of pink, carmine-red edge, underside pale-pink with purple tinge, green tips; C bright cyclamen-red, at the base white; medium-sized flower; upright grower; suitable for full sun.

Pabbe's Tudebekje 429
Single/semi-double; T carmine-pink with carmine-red stripes; S glossy strawberry-red, on the underside dull strawberry-red, small olive-green tips; C white with crimson veins; long slender flower; free-flowering; self-branching; upright grower; suitable for growing as pillar or climber; the edges of the sepals are grown together for 0.5 cm (0.2 in) at the base.

Pale Flame 219
Double; T white with pink blush and dark-pink stripes; S white with pink blush, at the base carmine-pink and carmine-pink edges, on the underside carmine-pink, small yellow-green tips; C bright purple-pink, fading to rose-red, at the base soft pink, dark rose-red edges and darker veins, irregular soft-pink splashes; large full flower; free-flowering; trailer; slow grower; intolerant of sun.

Palmengarten 275
Double; T carmine-pink; S carmine-red with small green tips; C deep-violet, at the base cyclamen-pink, red veins, the petaloids deep-violet with cyclamen-pink and carmine-pink splashes; rather large flower; reasonable flowering; self-branching; semi-trailer.

Pan 228
Single; T bright, pale robin-red with darker stripes; S bright robin-red, on the underside spiraea-pink, small green tips; C spiraea-red, at the base darker, dark-purple stripes; rather small flower held out; reasonable flowering; semi-trailer; needs a warm site in sheltered light; slow grower.

Panylla Prince 196
Single; T lavender-pink; S mauve-purple, on the underside purple; C mauve-purple, at the base white, purple edges and veins; very small flower; very floriferous; self-branching; upright grower; suitable for growing as a miniature standard or miniature pyramid; resistant to red spider mite.

Papa Bleuss 212
Double; T ivory-white with green tinge and red stripes; S white with red blush from base, on the underside candy-pink to bright pink, green tips; C bright violet-purple, maturing to purple-blue, at base bright pink, red veins; large flower; free-flowering; upright lax flower; can be grown as semi-trailer; for filtered light.

Parel van Waanrode 402
Single; T glossy waxy-white with pink tinge and pink stripes; S pale rose-red, on the underside light rose-red, green tips; C robin-red maturing to cardinal-red, at the base light rose-red, red veins and orange-pink splash; medium-sized flower; very floriferous; semi-trailer; for filtered light.

Passing Cloud 297
Single; T light rose-red; S splashy light rose-red to the lighter, green tips; C violet-purple, fading to mauve-purple, at the base rose-red, darker edges, dark-pink veins and rose-red splashes; rather large flower; free-flowering; self-branching; upright bushy grower; for full sun; suitable as a standard; easy to grow.

Paulus 242
Single; T light pink with green tinge; S on the upper side light vermillion-red shading to vermillion-pink towards the tip, scarlet-red edges, on the underside orange-red, shading to pale tomato-red towards the green tips; C tomato-red with bright red edge; medium-sized flower; upright grower; suitable for growing as a standard.

Peppermint Candy 64
Double; T soft pink; S soft pink, on the underside vivid pink, green tips; C lavender-pink, at the base pink, soft pink with lavender-pink-splashed petaloids; medium-sized flower; trailer.

Perry Park 158
Single; T waxy-white with pink blush and a touch of green; S white with pink blush, lighter towards the tips, on the underside splashy crimson, light-green tips; C cyclamen-red, at the base white, darker veins and pink splash; medium-sized flower; very floriferous; bushy growing semi-trailer; for full sun; suitable for containers.

Petit Four 177
Single; T pale purple-pink with darker splashes, S pale purple-pink, on the underside darker, yellow-green tips; C purple-red, at the base purple-pink; small flower; free-flowering over a long period; self-branching; semi-trailer; tolerates heat.

Petra de Groot 359
Single; T glossy cerise-red; S glossy cerise-red with darker veins; C deep blue-purple, maturing to violet, at the base cerise-red and from base cerise-red veins; rather small flower; free-flowering; upright bushy grower.

Piccolo 92
Single; T waxy-white with pink and green tinge; S waxy-white with pink tinge, on the underside white with lilac blush, green tips; C deep-purple, at the base carmine-pink, darker edges; small flower held out; very floriferous, flowering early and over a long period; self-branching; upright grower; for filtered light; suitable for growing as a pyramid.

Pieroy Liegois 241
Single; T glossy white with deep robin-red tinge and blush; S rose-red with green tips; C deep robin-red; medium-sized flower; upright grower.

Pink Jade 70
Single; T glossy crimson; S shading towards the green tips from crimson to light carmine-pink; C bright pink, at the base carmine-red, carmine-red veins; medium-sized flower; very floriferous; self-branching; upright grower; requires filtered light.

Pink Most 22
Double; T greenish-white with green stripes; S greenish-white with at the base a touch red, green tips; C palest pink, at the base pale carmine-pink, carmine-pink veins; large flower; free-flowering; upright grower; for filtered light.

Pink Quartette 447
Semi-double; T pink; S deep rose-red with vivid green tips; C white with rose-red veins; large flower; upright somewhat stiff grower.

Pink Slippers 83
Single; T waxy-white with green tinge; S waxy-white, at the base a touch pink, light-green tips; C soft lavender-pink, at base white, darker edges, dark-pink veins; medium-sized flower; free-flowering; self-branching; trailer; needs a cool site in filtered light or semi-shade.

Pio Pico 277
Double; T pink with darker blush; S very soft pink, on the underside light purple-pink, green tips; C purple-violet, maturing to red-purple; the petaloids have many soft-pink splashes; very large flower; reasonable flowering for such a large flower; trailer.

Playford 188
Single; T soft pink; S on the upper side soft pink, on the underside light carmine-pink, green tips; C bluish-mauve, at the base soft pink; rather small flower; very floriferous; upright grower; likes a shaded place, tolerates heat; best colour in shade; suitable for growing as a standard.

Pluto 370
Single/semi-double; T strawberry-red with darker stripes; S strawberry-red, to the tips lighter, on the underside vivid rose-red, small green tips; C dull purple, maturing to mauve-purple, at base vivid rose-red, darker edge, red veins; medium-sized flower; very floriferous; self-branching; semi-trailer; requires filtered light.

President 335
Single; T rose-red with paler blush; S rose-red with green tips; C robin-red, at base scarlet-red, darker edges, scarlet veins; rather large flower; free-flowering; self-branching; lax upright grower; can be grown as standard or as trailer; for full sun; hardy.

President Elliot 323
Single; T currant-red; S on the upper side glossy currant-red, on the underside dull currant-red; C purplish-red; medium-sized flower; free-flowering; bushy upright grower; also known under the name Rev. Elliot.

Pride of the West 184
Single; T pale carmine-pink; S carmine-pink, green tips; C cyclamen-purple, at the base carmine-pink, reddish edges and veins; rather long bell-shaped flower; free- and early-flowering; semi-trailer; needs early and careful pinching; for full sun; can be grown as an espalier.

Profusion 371
Single; T glossy strawberry-red; S glossy strawberry-red, green tips; C violet-purple, at the base crimson, crimson veins; rather small flower; free-flowering; branches well; upright bushy grower.

R

Radings Mia 73
Single; T pink-purple; S pink-purple, on the underside bright pink; C pink, at the base darker, darker edges and carmine-red veins; very small flower; free-flowering; upright grower; for full sun; fuchsia with red branches.

R.A.F. 256
Double; T deep-red; S deep-red, on the underside deep rose-red; C soft-pink, at the base rose-red, purple-red veins and pink splash; medium-sized flower; free-flowering; self-branching; upright grower; suitable for growing as a standard; needs a lot of pinching; looks like 'Fascination', but is better.

Rakker 239
Single; T soft-pink; S soft-pink, pale-green tips; C crimson, at the base light-pink; small flower; upright grower; tolerates full sun; can be grown as 'table'-standard.

Ray Maslin 249
Double; T white with green stripes and green tinge; S splashy cyclamen-pink, on the underside vivid appleblossom pink, shading to white towards the tips, small green tips; C cyclamen-purple, fading to red-purple, at base white, red veins with lilac splash; large flower; reasonable flowering; trailer; requires a sheltered position and filtered light.

Rayen 58
Double; T greenish-white with green stripes; S white with green tips; C splashy violet-blue with lighter streak over the petals; large flower; trailer.

Razzle Dazzle 211
Double; T pale pink; S pale pink, on the underside somewhat darker; C violet- and blue-purple, at the base pink, white edges, obvious red stripes; large flower; late and reasonable flowering; self-branching; needs a warm and sheltered place in filtered light.

Rebecca Williamson 498
Double; T waxy-white with light-pink faint and green stripes; S light-rose-red, on the underside rose-red, green tips; C crimson-pink, at the base rose-red, darker veins and rose-red splash; large flower; semi-trailer; requires a cool site in filtered light; suitable for baskets and standards; needs careful pinching.

Red Ace 286
Double; T crimson; S wine-red, on the underside crimson; C robin-red, fading to purple-red, at the base crimson, red veins; medium-sized flower; free-flowering; self-branching; upright grower; for full sun; suitable for growing as a standard.

Reichards Sämling 80
Single; T waxy-white with green tinge and stripes; S waxy-white with green tinge, on the underside white with pink tinge, green tips; C candy-pink, at the base white, darker veins, from base a white splash along the veins; medium-sized flower; very floriferous; self-branching; upright grower; dwarf; for full sun; lovely fuchsia, suitable for growing as a standard.

Renée 408
Single; T waxy-white with green stripes and pink blush; S waxy-white, on the underside with pink tinge, light-green tips; C cerise-red, maturing to faded red, deep-red edges, darker veins with pale-pink splash; medium-sized flower; very floriferous; self-branching; upright grower; sun-tolerant.

Rieksken Boland 372
Double; T white with green faint, green and pink grooves; S on the upper side crimson-pink with darker stripes, on the underside deep crimson-pink, green tips; C dark-aubergine-coloured, maturing to dark robin-red, at the base somewhat lighter, red veins; medium-sized flower; very free-flowering; trailer; needs a cool site in filtered light; can also be grown as a standard.

Robbie 26
Single; T pale-crimson-pink; S pale-crimson shading to white towards the tips, green tips; C white with pale crimson-pink veins; medium-sized flower; upright bushy grower with short joints; needs careful pinching to get in full bloom.

Robin 260
Double; T carmine-pink; S carmine-pink shading to white towards the tips, small green tips, on the underside carmine-pink; C violet-purple with pink splashes; rather large flower; trailer.

Robin Pacey 398
Single; T pale-rose-red; S carmine-pink, green tips; C lilac, maturing to deep purple-violet, at the base pale pink, red veins; rather large flower; free- but late- flowering; upright grower; for filtered light.

Rocket Fire 261
Double; T carmine-pink; S carmine-pink, on the underside somewhat lighter, small green tips; C blue-purple, the inner-petals are dark-pink, at the base pink; large flower; lax upright grower; can be grown as trailer.

Roesse Anja 180
Single; T crimson-purple with bright red stripes; S vivid rose-red with robin-red stripes, on the underside robin-red, green tips; C plum-purple, at the base red, plum-purple edges and red stripe in the centre; medium-sized flower; upright grower; for filtered light; red branches with long internodes.

Roesse Femke 187
Single; T white with green faint and pink blush; S pale crimson with carmine-pink streak through the centre, on the underside splashy carmine-red to carmine-pink, small green tips; C light lavender-purple fading to lilac-purple, obvious red stripes with palest lavender-purple splash; large flower; free-flowering; self-branching; trailer; for filtered light.

Roesse Marie 56
Semi-double; T palest pink; S palest pink, on the underside slightly darker; C lavender-blue; medium-sized flower; semi-trailer; for filtered light.

Roesse Mieke 139
Double; T white with green faint and stripes; S white with light pink blush, on the underside orchid-pink, green tips; C mauve-purple, maturing to purple-pink, at the base white, purple-pink edge, broad light streak through the centre from the petals; large flower; reasonable flowering; self-branching; semi-trailer; for filtered light.

Roesse Ministar 245
Single; T green with purple-blush; S on the upper side light-purple, to the tips changing to soft yellow-green, on the underside fuchsia-purple; C deep-aubergine-coloured, maturing to beet-root-red, at the base bright fuchsia-purple; small flower; free-flowering; self-branching; upright grower; for filtered light; strong fuchsia.

Roesse Mondy 68
Single; T yellow-green; S bright pink; C violet, at the base white; smallish flower held out; free-flowering; self-branching; upright bushy grower; for filtered light.

Roesse Rowin 142
Single; T white with aubergine-coloured stripes; S on the upper side light yellow-green, on the underside greenish-white; C deep blue-purple; large flower; semi-trailer; for filtered light; needs careful pinching.

Roesse Tricolor 141
Semi-double/double; T white with greenish touch; S on the upper side splashy pale candy-pink with cyclamen-pink splashes, on the underside carmine-pink with red blush, green tips; C deep purple-violet, at the base white, red veins and purple splash, large and small petaloids; large flower; free-flowering; self-branching; semi-trailer; for filtered light and sheltered site; suitable for growing as a pillar.

Roesse Wega 102
Single; T white with green tinge; S light shell-pink, on the underside appleblossom-pink; C bright fuchsia-purple, purple-pink edges and veins, bright pink splashes; medium-sized flower; semi-trailer; for filtered light.

Roesse Willem 103
Semi-double; T light-green with darker stripes; S on the upper side absinth-green, at base carmine-red blush, on the underside from base changing from carmine-red to absinth-green, olive-green tips; C violet-blue, maturing to purple-violet, at the base carmine-red, violet-blue edges, red veins and lilac splash; medium-sized flower; free-flowering; self-branching; trailer; for semi-shade.

Rogier de Groot 97
Single; T white with touch of green and pink blush; S at the base carmine-red shading to white towards the tip, on the underside crimson; C blue-violet, maturing to purple-violet, at the base phlox-pink, blue-violet edges, carmine-pink veins with phlox-pink splash; medium-sized flower; self-branching; upright grower; for filtered light.

Roland Desiré 360
Single; T carmine-pink with darker stripes; S carmine-pink with lighter splashes, green tips; C deep-purple; medium-sized flower; semi-trailer.

Roland von Bremen 120
Double; T white with green blush and green stripes; S white with small green tips; C blue-violet, white edges, at the base white; medium-sized flower; semi-trailer.

Romance 40
Double; T white; S white with green tips, on the underside soft-pink; C blue-violet, at base pale pink, the outer petals are pale-pink; large flower; reasonable flowering; trailer.

Rosalie 290
Single; T glossy crimson; S glossy crimson, on the underside cerise-red; C soft-pink, at the base cerise-red, obvious red veins; rather small flower; very floriferous; self-branching; upright grower; tolerant of full sun; suitable for growing as a standard; strong plant; makes dark-purple berries.

Rose Aylett 269
Double; T pale carmine-red; S pale carmine-red, on the underside carmine-red; C lavender-blue fading to lavender-purple, red veins; large flower; flowers well; upright bushy grower; can be grown as semi-trailer.

Rose City 105
Double; T white; S white with green tips; C lilac, at the base pink, pink splashes; large flower; trailer.

Rose Phenomenal 349
Double; T glossy scarlet; S scarlet; C light violet-purple, maturing to mauve-purple, at the base pink, red veins with pink splash; large flower; free-flowering; upright grower; for filtered light.

Ross Lea 403
Double; T glossy crimson; S glossy crimson, on the underside crimson; C deep purple; medium-sized flower; free-flowering; lax upright grower; suitable as semi-trailer.

Royal and Ancient 38
Single; T light pink with darker stripes; S appleblossom-pink, on the underside darker, vivid appleblossom-pink, large green tips; C light spiraea, at the base white, faint white veins; medium-sized flower; flowers late in the season; self-branching; upright grower; for filtered light.

Rozientje 41
Single/semi-double; T coral-pink with rose-red stripes; S pink, at base darker, underside carmine-red, green tips; C vivid appleblossom pink with obvious red stripes; medium-sized flower; free-flowering; self-branching; trailer; for full sun.

Ruddigor 482
Single; T bright orange-red; S on the upper side orange-red, on the underside vermillion-red, light-green tips; C sorb-apple-red, at base orange-red; medium-sized flower; free-flowering; upright grower; for full sun.

Rufus 336
Single; T crimson; S crimson with green tips; C crimson, at base carmine-red; medium-sized flower; very floriferous; self-branching; upright bushy grower; for full sun; can be grown as a standard; in the past known under the wrong name 'Rufus the Red'.

Sally Ann 250
Double; T white; S white with pink blush, on the underside carmine-pink, green tips; C bright red, at base white, darker edges and veins with coral-pink splashes; large flower; free-flowering; semi-trailer; for filtered light.

Sampson's Delight 205
Single/semi-double; T ivory-white with pink flush and pink stripes; S soft pink, on the underside rose-red, small green tips; C vivid rose-purple, at the base rose-red, red veins; medium-sized flower; free-flowering; semi-trailer; suitable for a standard and trailer; for full sun.

Santa Paula 404
Double; T carmine-red; S carmine-red with lighter splashes, shading to white towards the small green tips; C deep-purple, at base carmine-red; rather large flower; upright grower.

Scarborough Starshine 157
Single; T white with violet blush and stripes; S on the upper side white with violet-pink blush, on the underside white; C purple-violet, at the base soft pink; medium-sized flower; free-flowering; upright grower.

Schildehof 307
Semi-double; T crimson with darker stripes; S crimson, on the underside candy-pink, small green tips; C blue-violet, maturing to violet, darker edge, at the base red, red veins and carmine-red splash; medium-sized flower; free-flowering; upright grower; red horizontal-growing branches; for filtered light; can be grown as pyramid.

Schneewittchen 442
Single; T glossy rose-red with cerise-red veins; S crimson, small green tips; C white, at base crimson and crimson veins; rather small flower; very floriferous; upright grower.

Seventh Heaven 499
Double; T greenish white, green stripes; S on the upper side white with pink splashes, on the underside pale pink, dark-pink tips; C deep mauve-purple, at the base orange and white, mauve-purple edge, orange veins, many orange-red petaloids; large full flower; trailer; needs filtered light; lovely flower.

Sheila Crooks 393
Double; T glossy cerise-red; S glossy cerise-red with yellow-green tips; C blue-violet, at the base white; medium-sized flower; free-flowering; upright bushy grower.

Silver Dawn 57
Double; T waxy-white; S waxy-white, on the underside spiraea-pink, green tips; C light lavender-purple, fading to lavender-pink, at the base soft-pink, pink veins with faint pink splash; large full flower; free-flowering; upright grower; for full sun; needs careful pinching.

Silver Dollar 3
Single; T white; S white with vivid-pink blush, underside with a touch pink, green tips; C ivory-white; medium-sized flower; very floriferous; self-branching; for filtered light and semi-shade; can be grown as small standard; splendid white fuchsia.

Silver Wings 282
Double; T rose-red with darker stripes; S vivid rose-red, on the underside deeper coloured; C violet-pink; medium-sized flower; trailer.

Sinter Maarten 154
Single; T light absinth-green; S light pale absinth-green with touch cream, green tips; C phlox-pink, at base white, purple-red veins; long slender flower; very floriferous; self-branching; trailer; for filtered light; flowers as a cascade on the end of the branches.

Slippery Horn 151
Single; T white with bright pink blush; S white with bright pink blush; C candy-pink; long slender flower; free-flowering; trailer.

Software 66
Double; T white with green blush and green stripes; S white with pink blush, green stripes; underside white with pink blush; C lilac, fading to purple, at the base white, faint red veins; large full flower; self-branching; trailer; needs filtered light or semi-shade.

Soleil du Luxembourg 326
Single/semi-double; T glossy cerise-red; S crimson, small green tips; C cyclamen-purple, at the base carmine-red, reddish edges, red veins and carmine-red splash; medium-sized flower; very free-flowering; self-branching; trailer; for filtered light; can also be grown as a standard; flowers in terminal racemes.

Solmäs 295
Semi-double; T crimson with darker grooves; S light crimson, green tips; C bright violet, through the centre white with pink blush; trailer.

Sonata 450
Double; T white with pink blush and green stripes; S on the upper side appleblossom-pink, at the base darker, on the underside candy-pink, towards the tip becoming lighter, green tips; C clear white, at the base candy-pink and candy-pink veins; large full flower; trailer; sun-tolerant; branches break easily.

Sophie Claire 475
Single; T vivid pink with crimson grooves; S vivid pink, becoming lighter towards the green tips; C dark pink to salmon-coloured; medium-sized flower; upright grower.

Sophie's Surprise 472
Single; T peach-coloured with light crimson grooves; S light peach-coloured with green tips, on the underside slightly darker; C deep apricot-coloured; medium-sized flower; upright grower.

Squadron Leader 11
Double; T white; S white; C white with pink blush; medium-sized flower; self-branching; lax upright grower; suitable for growing for baskets.

St Anne 8
Semi-double; T white with carmine-red blush and grooves; S white with carmine-red blush, underside splashy pink, light green tips; C ivory-white with pink veins; medium-sized flower; self-branching; trailer; for filtered light; beautiful trailer with gold-variegated foliage and red branches.

Stad Ommen 119
Double; T white with yellow-green blush; S white, underside white with yellow-green blush; C purple-violet, the outer petals with obvious pink stripes; medium-sized flower; self-branching; lax upright grower; for a shaded site.

Star Eyes 251
Double; T light-pink with yellow-green stripes; S vivid rose-red, underside rose-red; C purple, at the base rose-red, rose-red veins with a single pale splash; large flower; trailer; for full sun.

Steeley 140
Double; T white with magenta stripes; S white, on the underside with light magenta flush, green tips; C dark violet, at base soft-pink, rose-red veins with soft-pink splashes; large very full flower; free-flowering; self-branching; trailer; for semi-shade.

Stella Marina 116
Semi-double; T deep-pink; S deep-pink to the tips becoming darker; C violet-blue with pink and white splashes; large flower; free-flowering; trailer.

Stientje Leget 406
Semi-double; T white with light carmine-pink blush; S white with light carmine-pink flush; C bright tomato-red, at the base soft-pink splashes; medium-sized flower; trailer.

Stolze von Berlin 438
Double; T bright strawberry-red; S bright strawberry-red; C clear white, at the base bright red, bright red veins; rather large flower; free-flowering; lax upright grower; can be grown as a standard and as trailer.

Subliem 240
Single/semi-double; T light carmine-pink with darker stripes; S light carmine-pink with darker stripes, orange flush, green tips; C robin-red, at the base light carmine-pink; medium-sized flower; free-flowering; self-branching; semi-trailer; for a sheltered site in filtered light.

Sulamith 364
Single; T glossy deep-red; S glossy deep-red with currant-red stripes; C dark plum-red, maturing to reddish-purple; small bell-shaped flower; very floriferous; self-branching; upright grower; for filtered light.

Susan Green 254
Single; T glossy white with soft-pink blush; S on the upper side from base to tips shading from soft carmine-pink to white, on the underside soft crimson-pink, green tips; C deep carmine-pink, at the base slightly lighter; medium-sized flower; upright grower; tolerates full sun.

Svenny 178
Single; T bright rose-red; S bright soft-pink, at base darker rose-red, on the underside carmine-pink, green tips; C fuchsia-purple, at the base carmine-pink, red veins with carmine-red splash; medium-sized flower; free-flowering; self-branching; upright grower; requires filtered light; suitable for growing as a standard or pillar.

Sweet Serenade 172
Double; T pink with darker stripes; S vivid-pink, on the underside vivid pink lighter towards the tips; C violet with pink splashes; large flower; reasonable flowering; lax upright grower or semi-trailer; suitable for baskets.

Sylvia Barker 410
Single; T white; S waxy-white, green tips; C smoky scarlet, at the base soft apricot-coloured; medium-sized flower; very floriferous; semi-trailer.

T

Taatje 99
Single/semi-double; T glossy cream-white flushed with green and with purple stripes; S purple-pink with mauve-purple blush and stripes, on the underside mauve-purple, large green tips; C deep-violet, at the base robin-red, red veins; rather small flower; very floriferous; self-branching; trailer; for filtered light; gives a cascade of bloom.

Task Force 156
Single; T white; S on the upper side white, on the underside white with lilac blush, green tips; C cyclamen-red fading to magenta, at the base soft-pink; large flower; vigorous upright grower; needs careful pinching.

Television 117
Double; T white with rose-red stripes; S white, on the underside soft-pink; C orchid-blue with rose-red splashes, at the base white; medium-sized flower; free-flowering; semi-trailer.

Thamar 48
Single; T white flushed with green; S white with pink blush, light-green tips; C light violet, fading to light purple, at the base somewhat white and with a white splash from the base; fairly small flower held out; very floriferous; self-branching; upright grower; tolerates full sun; strong fuchsia.

The Speedbird 115
Single/semi-double; T white, pink flush, red stripes; S white, at the base a touch of red, on the underside white pink flushed, green tips; C deep blue-purple, maturing to purple-violet, at the base white, darker edges, darker veins; medium-sized flower; free-flowering-self-branching; upright grower; for filtered light.

The Aristocrat 25
Double; T ivory-white with green flush and stripes; S cyclamen-pink with darker edges, on the underside vivid, dark appleblossom-pink, green tips; C cyclamen-pink, carmine-pink veins; large flower; free-flowering; upright grower; tolerates full sun; can be grown as a standard.

Theseus 320
Single; T glossy strawberry-red; S crimson; C cardinal-red with darker veins; medium-sized flower; free-flowering; semi-trailer; tolerates full sun.

Tijl Uilenspiegel 127
Double; T white with green stripes; S white with pink blush, on the underside pink, green tips; C blue-violet, at base pink, red veins and pale-pink splash; fairly small flower; very floriferous; self-branching; upright grower; for filtered light.

Tomma 325
Single; T rose-red; S rose-red, on the underside strawberry-red, yellow-green tips; C deep-red, at base rose-red, faint darker veins; medium-sized flower; free-flowering; self-branching; upright grower; for full sun; suitable for a standard.

Topspin 220
Single; T dark-pink; S carmine-pink, underside candy-pink, pale yellow-green tips; C light cardinal-red; small flower held out; free-flowering; creeping; for filtered light; suitable for baskets.

Torville and Dean 12
Double; T greenish-white with darker stripes; S creamy-white flushed green, on the underside cream-white with large green tips; C cream-white, at the base pink, pink veins; medium-sized flower; free-flowering; semi-trailer; for full sun; can be grown as 'half' standard.

Tosca 278
Double; T carmine-pink; S crimson with small green tips; C light lavender-pink, at the base crimson, crimson veins with faint pink splashes; large flower; fairly free-flowering; semi-trailer; for full sun; can be grown for baskets.

Trientje 72
Single; T light lavender-purple with darker stripes; S purple flushed with green, on the underside lilac-purple, green tips; C purple maturing to purple-violet, at the base white; small erect flower; very floriferous; self-branching; upright grower; for filtered light; can be grown as a standard or pillar; lovely fuchsia with glossy black berries.

Tropicana 252
Double; T cream with yellow-green flush; S pale pink, underside salmon-pink, green tips; C bright orange-red, fading to robin-red, at the base strawberry-red, red veins and dull red splash; large full flower; very free-flowering; trailer; for filtered light.

Troubadour 268
Double; T glossy scarlet-red with darker stripes; S scarlet-red, on the underside strawberry-red; C blue-violet fading to purple-violet, at the base strawberry-red, strawberry-red veins; large flower; upright grower.

Truus Gottmer 200
Single; T red-purple; S red-purple shading to yellow-green tip; C dark-aubergine-coloured; long slender flower; self-branching; trailer.

Turandot 123
Double; T waxy-white with green flush; S white with purple flush, green tips; C deep-purple-violet, fading to red-violet, at the base pinkish-white, white veins with soft-pink splash; medium-sized flower; reasonable flowering; self-branching; upright grower; for filtered light.

Two Tiers 193
Double; T light azalea-pink; S light azalea-pink, underside deeper coloured; C pale-violet, at the base white; fairly large flower; lax upright grower; can be grown in any shape, but splendidly suitable for baskets; very unusual with the petaloids sticking out of the corolla.

U, V

Uranus 397
Single; T glossy bright red; S glossy bright red, dark-red tips; C dark plum-purple, maturing to robin-red, at the base red, red veins and deep-red splash; medium-sized flower; very floriferous; self-branching; upright grower; for filtered light; an improved 'Gruss aud dem Bodethal'.

Vicmarther 308
Double; T carmine-red with darker stripes; S bright carmine-pink, light-green tips; C violet maturing to purple-violet, at the base light-pink, red veins with light-pink splash; fairly large flower; self-branching; for filtered light; suitable for a standard or pillar.

Victoria 405
Double; T bright crimson; S crimson; C deep-purple, at the base crimson; rather large flower; upright grower.

Victorian 16
Double; T glossy white flushed with pink, darker stripes; S white with soft-pink blush, on the underside soft-pink, green tips; C white with pink veins; rather large flower; fairly free-flowering; self-branching; upright grower; for filtered light.

Ville de Liège 263
Double; T waxy-red; S waxy-red; C violet-purple, maturing to red-purple, on the underside vivid rose-red, red veins and rose-red splash; medium-sized flower; very floriferous; self-branching; upright grower; requires filtered light.

Violetkoningin 146
Semi-double; T white with red blush; S white with crimson blush, on the underside pink, green tips; C blue-purple, maturing to red-purple, at the base red-purple; medium-sized flower; free-flowering; self-branching; trailer.

Violette Szabo 420
Single; T white flushed with green and pink; S white with pink blush, on the underside soft-pink; C smoky red-purple; medium-sized bell-shaped flower; free-flowering; self-branching; upright grower.

W

Walz Bugel 342
Single/semi-double; T bright red with darker stripes; S bright red with small green tips; C robin-red, at the base lighter, purple-red veins and faint red splash; early- and fairly free-flowering; requires a site in filtered light; needs careful pinching.

Walz Lucifer 77
Single; T cyclamen-pink with vivid pink stripes; S cyclamen-pink, green tips; C light tomato-red with darker veins; long slender flower; very floriferous; semi-trailer; for full sun.

Walz Piano 314
Single T strawberry-red; S carmine-pink, at the base strawberry-red, light-green tips; C light purple-red, at base red, striking red streak through the centre; long slender flower; free- and early-flowering; self-branching; semi-trailer; requires a light place out of the sun; needs careful pinching early in the season.

Walz Toorts 233
Single; T candy-pink with darker rose-red stripes; S on the upper side crimson, on the underside strawberry-red, small green tips; C flaming red, darker veins with scarlet splash; long flower held out; very floriferous; upright grower; for full sun; needs a lot of careful pinching; triphylla-type.

Walz Trompet 313
Single; T deep-red with darker stripes; S scarlet-red with bright green tips; C robin-red, at the base Turkish red, darker veins and Turkish-red splash; very floriferous; flowers early and over a long period; self-branching; upright grower; for full sun.

Walz Tuba 312
Single; T crimson; S bright red, on the underside cerise-red, large green tips; C purple-pink, at the base cerise-red, fuchsia-purple veins with red splash; medium-sized flower; free-flowering; self-branching; trailer; for full sun.

Waltzing Matilde 36
Double; T pale-pink; S light-pink on the upper side, on the underside pink, green tips; C pale-pink; medium-sized flower; tolerates heat but in a shaded place; best colour however in bright light.

Wapenvelds Bloei 221
Single; T fuchsia-purple; S mauve-pink, at the base fuchsia-purple, green tips; C light robin-red, red veins and vivid rose-red splash; small flower; very floriferous; self-branching; upright grower.

Waveney Gem 101
Single; T porcelain-white flushed with pink; S on the upper side porcelain-white flushed with pink, on the underside cyclamen-pink, small green tips; C purple, fading to cyclamen-purple, at the base cyclamen-pink; very floriferous; self-branching; semi-trailer; sun-tolerant.

Waveney Sunrise 190
Single; T light-pink; S light-pink with darker blush, yellow-green tips; C violet, at the base light-pink; upright grower.

Westminster Chimes 396
Single/semi-double; T carmine-red; S carmine-red, underside rose-red, small green tips; C bright violet, maturing to purple, at the base light rose-red, red veins and soft-pink splash; fairly small flower held out; very floriferous; self-branching; semi-trailer; for filtered light.

Whiteknight's Blush 42
Single; T shell-pink; S pale pink, on the underside orchid-pink, yellow-green tips; C phlox-purple; fairly small flower; free-flowering; self-branching; bushy upright grower; will take full sun.

Wiebke Becker 5
Single; T white with pink blush and dark-pink stripes; S clear white flushed with pink along the edge at the base, underside white with pink at the base, green tips; C clear white with small pink veins; medium-sized flower; free-flowering; trailer; for filtered light.

Wieth 300
Single; T light carmine-pink with carmine-pink stripes; C on the upper side shading from base from crimson to soft-pink, on the underside candy-pink, small green tips; C purple-mauve, at the base clear pink, purple-mauve edges and veins; fairly large flower; reasonable flowering; semi-trailer; for full sun.

Wilson's Joy 166
Single; T white; S white, flushed pink on the underside; C light plum-purple, white at the base; medium-sized flower; free-flowering; upright grower.

Wilson's Pearls 451
Single/semi-double; T carmine-red; S carmine-red; C white, at the base carmine-red, carmine-red veins with pink splash; medium-sized flower; free-flowering; trailer; takes full sun.

Win Oxtoby 67
Single; T white with pink blush and dark-pink stripes and grooves; S pink; C salmon-pink; medium-sized flower; semi-trailer.

Wingrove's Mammoth 449
Double; T crimson; S glossy crimson; C white, at the base crimson, pronounced red stripes; large flower; flowers late; upright grower.

Woodnook 137
Double; T waxy-white with green flushed and green stripes; S waxy-white flushed with green, bright green tips; C lavender-purple, fading to lilac-purple, at the base pink, red veins and pink splash; medium-sized flower; free-flowering; self-branching; upright grower; for filtered light; can be grown as a standard.

Y, Z

Ymke 477
Single; T vivid rose-red with darker stripes; S vivid pink, on the underside vermillion-red, yellow-green tips; C bright orange-red, at the base vivid pink and vivid-pink veins; long slender flower; very floriferous; low upright grower; can be used as a bedding plant; triphylla-type.

Zaza 76
Single; T appleblossom-pink with darker stripes; S on the upper side shading from candy-pink to white, on the underside vivid rose-red, lighter towards the large green tips; C pale pink, at the base vivid rose-red; fairly small flower; free-flowering; semi-trailer; takes full sun.

Zet's Alpha 463
Single; T carmine-red with crimson stripes; S carmine-pink, at the base crimson, underside white to pale pink, yellow-green tips; C orange-red, at the base pale pink, darker veins; long slender flower; free-flowering; self-branching; upright grower; triphylla-type.

Zolder's Glorie 113
Double; T white green flushed; S white with pink blush; C deep-purple and white with purple striped, at the base pink; medium-sized flower; trailer.

Lists

500 fuchsias
arranged by colour and characteristics

All the fuchsias in this book, illustrated in the photographs on the preceding pages, are arranged in the lists which follow: first of all they are listed by colour, and then by other important characteristics. By using the lists you can see what fuchsia you need for particular requirements.

All the fuchsias have been described in alphabetical order, starting on page 63. After each description is the number of the relevant photograph. This way you can see how your fuchsia should turn out in practice.

White

Alkmaars Glorie
Alyce Larson
Bergerac
Bonsay
Carefree
Carla Johnson
Constellation
Ice Maiden
Igloo Maid
Linda Goulding
Montalba
Silver Dollar
Squadron Leader
St Anne
Torville and Dean
Victorian
Wiebke Becker

White/pink

Ann Pacey
Bled Lagon
Circus Spangles
De Groot's Robbedoes
Delta's Dream
Delta's Song
Finn
Frau Margot Heinke

Graf Spee
Hans Peter Peters
Hermie Kainz
Mrs Marshall
Nicky Veerman
Pink Most
Reichards Sämling
Sally Ann
Slippery Horn

White/lavender

Corsair
Gordon's China Rose
Heston Blue
Jandel
Jane Humber
Katie
Knights Errant
Lican Ray
Lorna Swinbank
Lütgerdina
Misty Haze
More Applause
My Dear
Olympic Lass
Pale Flame
Pink Slippers
Rose City
Silver Dawn
Software
Woodnook

White/purple

Ali Harder
Anna Pauline
Arels Zwaantje
Bella Rosella
Belvedere
Bettina
Bloemelingen
City of Adelaïde
Coachman Sämling
Crackerjack
Crusader

Crystal Blue
Dalli Dalli
David Ward
Dawn Star
Deborah
Deep Purple
Delta's Fair
Derby Star
Diadem
Docteur Charles Favier
Dutch Rosemarieke
Ebbtide
Ed Largarde
Elisabeth Göring
Elizabeth Honoré
English Rose
Erika Frohmann
Floretta
Fransca
Frederike
George Barr
Gleneagles
Glowing Lilac
Golden la Campanella
Grimbeerd
Grusz an Graz
Guurtje
Hanau
Hendrina Bovenschen
Hilchenbacher Grusz
Humboldt Holiday
Humiko Kamo
Imperial Fantasy
Jaspers Groentje
Joe Kusber
Koning Nobel
La Fiesta
Lidi
Lindsay Hendrickx
Mabejo
Maresi
Papa Bleuss
Perry Park
Piccolo
Rayen
Roesse Mieke
Roland von Bremen
Romance

Scarborough Sunshine
Seventh Heaven
Stad Ommen
Steeley
Task Force
Television
Thamar
The Speedbird
Tijl Uilenspiegel
Turandot
Violetkoningen
Violette Szabo
Waveney Gem
Zolder's Glorie

White/aubergine

Airdale
Lubbertje Hop
Wilson's Joy

White/red

Bolleken
British Jubilee
Dennis
El Tope
Florentina
Jülchen
Magic Flute
Ostfriesland
Pabbe's Blikoortje
Renée
Stientje Leget
Sylvia Barker

White/orange

Anita
Dolly's Day Dream

White/pink/pink

The Aristocrat

White/pink/orange

Win Oxtoby

White/pink/purple

Taatje

Pink

Angela
Berenvelt
Big Slim
Carmen Maria
Charles de Gaulle
Daddy Longleg
F. juntasensis
Fenman

Lee Antony
Linda Copley
Mon Amie
Rebecca Williamson
Royal and Ancient
Rozientje
Susan Green
Waltzing Matilde

Pink/white

Amie Josée Frans
Catharine Law
Citation
De Groot's Lady
Delicate White
Dolly Pausch
Gina
Hellas
Herjan de Groot
Kati
Kay Riley
Liebelei
Marylin Olsen
Medalist
Monte Rosa
Pink Quartette
Robbie
Sonata

Pink/lavender

Daniela
Danish Pastry
De Groot's Beauty
Fairy Tales
Hazel
Jaspers Wentelwiek
Joan Leach
Joanne
Kathy's Sparkler
Kit Oxtoby
Lavender Kate
Misty Blue
Montevideo
Peppermint Candy
Playford
Robin Pacey
Roesse Marie
Zaza

Pink/purple

Adriaan
Adriene Berger
Ajax
Alfred de Groot
Anneke
Bambini
Ben Hur
Berba's Impossible
Beryl's Choice
Bonita
Buga '91
Can Can
Canada
Cap Arcona

Charming
Church Town
Commander-in-Chief
Cyndy Robijn
Delta's Delight
Delta's Paljas
Delta's Sympfonie
Dulcie Elisabeth
Elsine
Festival
Flamenco Dancer
Fleur de Picardie
Frau Mint
Garden Boy
Garden Week
Geesche
George Johnson
Gerburg Emmerich
Gerhard Mathieu
Glockenspiel
Gracie
Green 'n Gold
Gwen Dodge
Hans van de Beek
Hercules
Hilda
Hölderlin
Isle of Mull
Italiano
Jaspers Duimelot
Jaspers Ringeling
Joan Gilbert
Ken Jennings
Kentish Maid
Kerry Ann
Leodien
Liesbeth Jansen
Lindisfarne
Little John
Mallemolen
Mama Bleuss
Margaret Rose
Martin's Leencor
Marty
Max Jaffa
Mia Goedman
Mrs Susan Brookfield
Palmengarten
Passing Cloud
Pio Pico
Pride of the West
Ray Maslin
Razzle Dazzle
Robin
Rocket Fire
Roesse Mondy
Roesse Tricolor
Roesse Wega
Roger Desiré
Samson's Delight
Silver Wings
Stella Marina
Svenny
Sweet Serenade
Two Tiers
Waveney Sunrise
Whiteknight's Blush
Wieth

Pink/aubergine

Janna Roddenhof
Long John
Mina Knudde
Parel van Waanrode
Petit Four
Pieroy Liegois
President
Rieksken Boland
Roesse Anja (pink/aub.)
Subliem (pink/aub.)

Pink/red

Ati
Che Bella
Cheers
De Groot's Pipes
Delta's Prelude
Erica Veldkamp
Five Times
Flor Izel
Gelre
Gert Jan Bekamp
Golden Jubilee
Goldsworth Beauty
Hendrik den Besten
Hendrina Josephina
Janna
Jaspers Vuurbal
Jean
Jeanette Schwab
Jess
Joker
Joyce Sinton
Katinka
Les Hobbs
Lilo Vogt
Marloesje ter Beek
Nici's Findling
Oriental Sunrise
Paulus
Rakker
Tomma
Topspin
Walz Lucifer
Walz Piano
Wapenvelds Bloei

Pink/orange

Brighton Belle
Glitters
Glowing Ambers
Golden Arrow
Jacques Grasborn
Ken Goldsmith
Kim Broekhof
Monty Python
Orangeblossom
Sophie Claire
Sophie's Surprise
Tropicana
Ymke

Pink/red/red

Walz Toorts

Rose-red

New Fascination

Rose-red/rose-purple

Jan van Maasakkers

Rose-red/pink

Keystone

Aubergine

Bertha Timmer
Janneke Brinkman-Salentijn

Aubergine/purple

Delta's Glorie

Aubergine/white

Earebarre
Herman de Graaff

Red

Alsace
Ashley
Banzai
Bas Weeda
California Saga
De Groot's Kruimel
F. fulgens var. *rubra grandiflora*
F. fulgens variegata
Firenzi
Herzelin
Huize Ruurlo
Insulinde
Jacqueline
Javelin
Len Bielby
Lottie Hobby
Martien van Vugt
Rufus
Theseus

Red/white

Arcadia Gold
Delta's Memory
Hanna
Kyoto
Leine Perle
Madame Cornelissen
Medusa
Merimbula Giant

Pabbe's Tudebekje
Schneewittchen
Stolze von Berlin
Wilson's Pearls
Wingrove's Mammoth

Red/pink

Annie den Otter
Bubble Hanger
Danny Boy
Emile de Wildeman
Geismar
Long Distance
Pink Jade
R.A.F.
Rosalie
Walz Tuba

Red/lavender

Kathy Louise
Lilac Dainty
Roesse Femke
Rose Ayet
Tosca

Red/purple

André le Nostre
Anna
Anne Marie
Apache
Armand Simmon
Belle de Limbourg
Birgitt Heincke
Bouvigne '91
Centenary
Circe
Comet
Cor Spek
Corallina var. tricolori
Corallina
Daniel Lambert
Daniëlle Frystein
David
Delta's Drop
Delta's Night
Die Fledermaus
Doctor S. A. Appel
Duke of York
Eden Beauty
Eden's Delight
Frau Hilde Ramenmacher
Frozen Tears
Geessien Not
Golden Multa
Grumpy
Haus Wiesengrund
Ingelore
Jeeves
Joan's Delight
Julia
Julicka
Karina
Königin der Frühe
Lavaglut

Lichtendorf
Lotterer Queen
Magilda
Mieke Meursing
Nuwenspete
Petra de Groot
Pluto
Profusion
Rogier de Groot
Rose Phenomenal
Ross Lea
Santa Paula
Schildehof
Sheila Crooks
Soleil de Luxembourg
Solmäs
Troubadour
Vicmarther
Victoria
Ville de Liège
Westminster Chimes

Red/aubergine

Alice Bayet
Croix d'Honneur
Gerharda's Aubergine
Japmar Hofmeyer
La Courneuve Fleury
Lidie Bartelink
Loch Lomond
Luscious
Monte Negro
Pan
President Elliot
Red Ace
Sulamith
Truus Gottmer
Uranus
Walz Bugel
Walz Trompet

Red/orange

Danny Kay
Engellina Schwab
Orange Glow

Red/pink/orange

Zet's Alpha

Orange

Obergärtner Koch

Orange/pink

Eternal Flame

Orange/red

Dutch Kingsize
Michel Schwab

Mieke Alferink
Ruddigor

Yellow-green

Martin's Yellow Surprise

Green/purple

Jan zonder Vrees
Roesse Robin
Roesse Willem

Green/pink

Sinter Maartin

Green/aubergine

Jaap Brummel
Martin's Catharina
Roesse Ministar

Cream/pink

Joop van Brakel

Cream/red

Jupiter Seventy

Lavender/pink

Mollie Beaulah
Mötti
Radings Mia

Lavender/purple

Lechlade Gorgon
Panylla Prince

Lavender/purple/purple

Trientje

Purple/red

Driesje van den Berg

Fuchsia species

F. fulgens var. rubra grandiflora (with
multicoloured foliage)
F. fulgens variegata
F. juntasensis

Primary crossings

Jeanette Schwab
Katinka
Lechlade Gorgon
Martin's Yellow Suprise
Michel Schwab

Triphylla-types

Ati
Brighton Belle
Golden Arrow
Insulinde
Jacqueline
Ken Goldsmith
Lee Antony
Len Bielby
Monty Python
Obergärtner Koch
Ymke
Zet's Alpha

Variegated foliage

Arcadia Gold
Armand Simmon
Charming
Corallina var. tricolori
Duke of York
F. fulgens var. rubra grandiflora (with
variegated foliage)
Golden la Campanella
Golden Multa
Green 'n Gold
Igloo Maid

Double fuchsias

Adriaan
Alsace
Alyce Larson
Amie Josée Frans
André le Nostre
Angela
Anna
Anne Marie
Anneke
Apache
Arcadia Gold
Armand Simmon
Bella Rosella
Belvedere
Ben Hur
Beryl's Choice
Birgitt Heincke
Bled Lagon
Bloemelingen
Bolleken
Born Free
Bonita
Bonsay
British Jubilee
Canada
Carefree
Catharine Law
Centenary

Cheers
Circus Spangles
City of Adelaïde
Commander-in-Chief
Constellation
Corsair
Crusader
Crystal Blue
Cyndy Robijn
Danny Boy
Danny Kaye
David Ward
Dawn Star
De Groot's Kruimel
Deborah
Deep Purple
Die Fledermaus
Dolly Pausch
Dolly's Day Dream
Dulcie Elisabeth
Ebbtide
Ed Lagarde
Emile de Wildeman
English Rose
Erica Veldkamp
Erika Fromann
Festival
Flamenco Dancer
Florentina
Flor Izel
Frau Hilde Radenmacher
Garden Boy
Garden Week
Gerhard Mathieu
Gina
Glockenspiel
Glowing Lilac
Golden Jubilee
Gracie
Guurtje
Hanna
Hazel
Hilchenbacher Grusz
Humboldt Holiday
Humiko Kamo
Ice Maiden
Igloo Maid
Imperial Fantasy
Italiano
Japp Brummel
Jandel
Jane Humber
Jaspers Vuurbal
Joan Gilbert
Joanne
Joe Kusber
Julie
Kathy Louise
Kathy's Sparkler
Kati
Kay Riley
Kit Oxtoby
La Fiesta
Lavender Kate
Lidi
Liesbeth Jansen
Lilac Dainty
Linda Copley
Luscious
Mabejo

Mama Bleuss
Marloesje ter Beek
Marty
Medalist
Merimbula Giant
Misty Blue
Misty Haze
Mollie Beaulah
Mon Amie
Monte Rosa
Montevideo
More Applause
Mrs. Susan Brookfield
My Dear
New Fascination
Olympic Lass
Pale Flame
Palmengarten
Papa Bleuss
Peppermint Candy
Pink Most
Pio Rico
R.A.F.
Ray Maslin
Rayen
Razzle Dazzle
Rebecca Williamson
Red Ace
Rieksken Boland
Robin
Rocket Fire
Roesse Mieke
Romance
Rose Phenomenal
Rose Ayet
Rose City
Ross Lea
Sally Ann
Santa Paula
Seventh Heaven
Sheila Crooks
Silver Dawn
Silver Wings
Software
Sonata
Squadron Leader
Stad Ommen
Star Eyes
Steeley
Stolze von Berlin
Sweet Serenade
Television
The Aristocrat
Tijl Uilenspiegel
Torville and Dean
Tosca
Tropicana
Troubadour
Turandot
Two Tiers
Vicmarther
Victoria
Victorian
Ville de Liège
Waltzing Matilde
Wingrove's Mammoth
Woodnook
Zolder's Glorie

Small-flowered fuchsias

Ali Harder
Bambini
Banzai
Bertha Timmer
Daniela
Daniëlle Frystein
David
Delta's Dream
Duke of York
Elsine
Floretta
Fransca
Geesien Not
George Barr
Golden Multa
Grumpy
Hendrina Josephina
Herzelin
Hölderlin
Jan zonder Vrees
Janneke Brinkman-Salentijn
Japmar Hofmeyer
Joan's Delight
Lidie Bartelink
Lilac Dainty
Little John
Lottie Hobby
Lütgerdina
Martin's Catharina
Mini
Mötti
My Dear
Orangeblossom
Pan
Panylla Prince
Petit Four
Petra de Groot
Piccolo
Profusion
Radings Mia
Roesse Mia
Roesse Ministar
Roesse Mondy
Schneewittchen
Taatje
Thamar
Topspin
Wapenvelds Bloei
Westminster Chimes
Whiteknight's Blush

Suitable for baskets

Adriaan
Alfred de Groot
Alice Bayet
Alkmaars Glorie
Alyce Lardson
Angela
Anne Marie
Anna Pauline
Anneke
Arels Zwaantje
Ati
Bella Rosella
Ben Hur
Berenvelt

Bergerac
Big Slim
Born Free
Bonita
British Jubilee
Bubble Hanger
Carefree
Circus Spangles
Coachman Sämling
Crackerjack
Croix d'Honneur
Crystal Blue
Cyndy Robijn
Danish Pastry
Danny Boy
Danny Kaye
De Groot's Beauty
De Groot's Kruimel
De Groot's Pipes
De Groot's Robbedoes
Deborah
Delta's Fair
Delta's Prelude
Docteur Charles Favier
Dolly Pausch
Ebbtide
Eden Beauty
Erica Veldkamp
Fairy Tales
Finn
Flamenco Dancer
Florentina
Flor Izel
Frau Margot Heinke
Frau Mint
Garden Boy
Gelre
Gerburg Emmerich
Gerharda's Aubergine
Gina
Glockenspiel
Glowing Ambers
Glowing Lilac
Golden Arrow
Golden Jubilee
Golden la Campanella
Golden Multa
Gracie
Graf Spee
Grimbeerd
Grusz an Graz
Guurtje
Hazel
Hendrina Jonephina
Herman de Graaff
Hermie Kainz
Hilchenbacher Grusz
Huize Ruurlo
Humboldt Holiday
Ice Maiden
Imperial Fantasy
Italiano
Jacques Grasborn
Jan van Maasakkers
Jane Humber
Japmar Hofmeyer
Jaspers Duimelot
Jaspers Wentelwiek
Jean

Jess
Joop van Brakel
Kathy's Sparkler
Katie
Kay Riley
Kim Broekhof
Kit Oxtoby
Koning Nobel
Lidie Bartelink
Lilo Vogt
Linda Copley
Lindsay Hendrickx
Little John
Loch Lomond
Long John
Luscious
Mabejo
Mama Bleuss
Maresi
Marloesje ter Beek
Martien van Vugt
Medusa
Merimbula Giant
Mina Knudde
Misty Haze
Monte Negro
Montevideo
More Applause
Mötti
Olympic Lass
Orangeblossom
Oriental Sunrise
Pale Flame
Peppermint Candy
Pio Pico
President
Rayen
Rebecca Williamson
Robin
Rocket Fire
Roesse Femke
Roesse Willem
Romance
Rose Ayet
Rose City
Rozientje
Samson's Delight
Silver Wings
Sinter Maarten
Slippery Horn
Soleil de Luxembourg
Solmäs
Sonata
Squadron Leader
St. Anne
Star Eyes
Steeley
Stella Marina
Stientje Leget
Stolze von Berlin
Sweet Serenade
Taatje
Topspin
Tosca
Tropicana
Two Tiers
Violetkoningen
Walz Bugel
Walz Lucifer

Walz Tuba
Wiebke Becker
Wilson's Pearls
Zolder's Glorie

Suitable as a standard

Ali Harder
Ann Pacey
Annie den Otter
Birgitt Heincke
California Saga
Daniel Lambert
De Groot's Lady
Diadem
Eden's Delight
Elisabeth Göring
Fleur de Picardie
George Barr
Gerhard Mathieu
Gerharda's Aubergine
Gwen Dodge
Hans Peter Peters
Haus Wiesengrund
Huize Ruurlo
Jandel
Javelin
Joe Kusber
Joyce Sinton
Kathy's Sparkler
Ken Jennings
Kentish Maid
Königen de Frühe
Lavaglut
Lechlade Gorgon
Linda Goulding
Lindisfarne
Lotterer Queen
Lütgerdina
Madame Cornelissen
Mama Bleuss
Mieke Meursing
Misty Haze
Mon Amie
New Fascination
Nicky Veerman
Orange Glow
Panylla Prince
Passing Cloud
Paulus
Playford
President
R.A.F.
Rakker
Rebecca Williamson
Red Ace
Reichards Sämling
Rieksken Boland
Rosalie
Rufus
Samson's Delight
Silver Dollar
Soleil de Luxembourg
Stolze von Berlin
Svenny
The Aristocrat
Tomma
Torville and Dean

Trientje
Two Tiers
Vicmarther
Woodnook

Suitable for training

Annie den Otter
Birgitt Heincke
El Tope
Elisabeth Göring
Geismar
Hölderlin
Javelin
Jean
Jülchen
Lavaglut
Linda Goulding
Lotterer Queen
Lubbertje Hop
Mieke Alferink
Montalba
Mrs. Marshall
Nici's Findling
Nicky Veerman
Pabbe's Tudebekje
Panylla Prince
Piccolo
Pride of the West
Roesse Tricolor
Schildehof
Svenny
Trientje
Two Tiers
Vicmarther

Dwarfs

Bambini
Daniela
Daniëlle Frystein
Ingelore
Joan Leach
Mini
Reichards Sämling

Hardy

Charming
Corallina
Corallina var. *tricolori*
Janna Roddenhof
Liesbeth Jansen
Lottie Hobby
Madame Cornelissen
Rufus

Difficult to over-winter or difficult to grow

Beryl's Choice
Cheers
Danny Boy
Garden Week
La Fiesta

Long John
Luscious

Easy to grow, strong plant

Ann Pacey
Annie den Otter
Arels Zwaantje
Bonita
California Saga
Carla Johnson
Charming
Commander-in-Chief
Croix d'Honneur
Daniëlle Frystein
Die Fledermaus
Dolly Pausch
Emile de Wildeman
Floretta
Frau Hilde Radenmacher
Gina
Gwen Dodge
Hanna
Kerina
Kerry Ann
Lichtendorf
Linda Goulding
Montalba
Passing Cloud
Piccolo
Roesse Ministar
Rosalie
Thamar

Suitable for sun

Alsace
Amie Josée Frans
Anna
Annie den Otter
Arcadia Gold
Armand Simmon
Berba's Impossible
Big Slim
Birgitt Heincke
British Jubilee
Brighton Belle
California Saga
Carla Johnson
Commander-in-Chief
Cor Spek
De Groot's Lady
De Groot's Beauty
De Groot's Robbedoes
Delta's Delight
Delta's Glorie
Delta's Night
Delta's Prelude
Delta's Song
Eden Beauty
Eden's delight
Engellina Schwab
Fairy Tales
Fenman
Flor Izel
Frau Hilde Radenmacher
Frau Margot Heinke

Geesche
Geismar
Gelre
Gerharda's Aubergine
Gert Jan Bekamp
Glitters
Green 'n Gold
Haus Wiesengrund
Herzelin
Hölderlin
Huize Ruurlo
Ingelore
Jacqueline
Jandel
Janna
Jaspers Duimelot
Jaspers Groentje
Jaspers Wentelwiek
Javelin
Jean
Joyce Sinton
Julia
Jülchen
Jupiter Seventy
Katinka
Keystone
Kit Oxtoby
Königin der Frühe
Kyoto
Lechlade Gorgon
Leine Perle
Len Bielby
Les Hobbs
Lidie Bartelink
Loch Lomond
Madame Cornelissen
Martien van Vugt
Mia Goedman
Mieke Alferink
Mon Amie
Mötti
New Fascination
Nici's Findling
Nicky Veerman
Orange Glow
Oriental Sunrise
Pabbe's Blikoortje
Pabbe's Tudebekje
Passing Cloud
Perry Park
Petit Four
President
Pride of the West
Rakker
Radings Mia
Red Ace
Reichards Sämling
Renée
Rosalie
Rozientje
Ruddigor
Rufus
Samson's Delight
Silver Dawn
Sonata
Star Eyes
Susan Green
Thamar
The Aristocrat

Theseus
Tomma
Torville and Dean
Tosca
Walz Lucifer
Walz Trompet
Walz Tuba
Waltzing Matilde
Waveney Gem
Whiteknight's Blush
Wieth
Wilson's Pearls
Zaza

Shade or filtered light

Adriaan
Adriene Berger
Ajax
Ali Harder
Anne Marie
Anna Pauline
Ann Pacey
Apache
Arels Zwaantje
Banzai
Bergerac
Bettina
Bouvigne '91
Can Can
City of Adelaïde
Croix d'Honneur
Crusader
Dalli Dalli
Daniela
Dawn Star
De Groot's Pipes
Delicate White
Diadem
Driesje van den Berg
Dutch Rosemarieke
Earebarre
El Tope
Elisabeth Göring
Elsine
Fleur de Picardie
Floretta
Fransca
Frozen Tears
Gerhard Mathieu
Gordon's China Rose
Grumpy
Guurtje
Hans van de Beek
Hellas
Hendrik den Besten
Hendrina Bovenschen
Humiko Kamo
Igloo Maid
Imperial Fantasy
Insulinde
Jaap Brummel
Jacques Grasborn
Jan van Maasakkers
Jan zonder Vrees
Jane Humber
Jaspers Ringeling
Joop van Brakel
Julicka

Kentish Maid
Kim Broekhof
La Fiesta
Lavaglut
Leodien
Lican Ray
Lichtendorf
Little John
Long Distance
Lotterer Queen
Lubbertje Hop
Lütgerdina
Magilda
Mallemolen
Mama Bleuss
Martin's Catharina
Max Jaffa
Medusa
Mieke Meursing
Mina Knudde
Monte Negro
Monty Python
More Applause
My Dear
Nuwenspete
Ostfriesland
Pan
Papa Bleuss
Parel van Waanrode
Piccolo
Pink Jade
Pink Most
Playford
Pluto
Razzle Dazzle
Robin Pacey
Roesse Anja
Roesse Femke
Roesse Marie
Roesse Mieke
Roesse Ministar
Roesse Mondy
Roesse Robin
Roesse Tricolor
Roesse Wega
Roesse Willem
Rogier de Groot
Rose Phenomenal
Royal and Ancient
Sally Ann
Schildehof
Seventh Heaven
Sinter Maarten
Software
Soleil de Luxembourg
St. Anne
Stad Ommen
Subliem
Sulamith
Taatje
The Speedbird
Tijl Uilenspiegel
Topspin
Trientje
Tropicana
Turandot
Uranus
Vicmarther
Victorian

Ville de Liège
Walz Bugel
Westminster Chimes
Wiebke Becker
Woodnook

Shade or cool and sheltered position

Alyce Larson
Ashley
Ati
Bas Weeda
Bella Rosella
Bertha Timmer
Beryl's Choice
Bubble Hanger
Canada
Carefree
Carmen Marie
Che Bella
Cheers
Citation
Constellation
Corallina
Corsair
Crackerjack
Crystal Blue
Danish Pastry
Dawn Star
Deborah
Delta's Drop
Delta's Fair
Delta's Memory
Delta's Paljas
Delta's Sympfonie
Dutch Kingsize
Ebbtide
Ed Lagarde
Elizabeth Honoré
Eternal Flame
Florentina
Frederike
Garden Week
Geesien Not
George Johnson
Glowing Ambers
Grusz an Graz
Hanau
Hazel
Herjan de Groot
Heston Blue
Humboldt Holiday
Ice Maiden
Isle of Mull
Italiano
Jandel
Janneke Brinkman-Salentijn
Joan Gilbert
Joan's Delight
Joe Kusber
Joker
Kathy Louise
Kathy's Sparkler
Kerry Ann
Lilo Vogt
Long John
Lorna Swinbank
Margaret Rose

Medalist
Merimbula Giant
Misty Haze
Mollie Beaulah
Mrs. Marshall

Pale Flame
Pink Slippers
Ray Maslin
Razzle Dazzle
Rebecca Williamson

Rieksken Boland
Roesse Tricolor
Silver Dollar
Steeley
Waltzing Matilde